WHY WE ARE SUPERNATURAL:

An Anthology of Strange Encounters

Compiled by Dakota Frandsen
Edited by Sara Larson

Bald and Bonkers Network LLC

Why We Are Supernatural: An Anthology of Strange Encounters

Published by: Revitalized Occult and Strange, an imprint of Bald and Bonkers Network LLC

ISBN: 979-8-3303-3079-9
EISBN: 979-8-3303-3080-5

First Printing, 2024

Table of Contents

The Call to Action

Have you ever had an encounter that defies explanation? Seen a ghost, spotted a UFO, or experienced something truly otherworldly? We want to hear your story!

"Why We Are Supernatural," organized by Dakota Frandsen and edited by Sara Larson, is an upcoming anthology that aims to share real supernatural encounters with the world. This unique collection will explore why people experience these mysterious phenomena and how they shape our lives and understanding of the unknown.

Published under the imprint Revitalized Occult and Strange by Bald and Bonkers Network LLC, this anthology is more than just a book; it's a community effort to bring together those who seek answers and those who have lived through inexplicable events. Your story could help someone else feel less alone in their experiences and contribute to a broader understanding of the supernatural.

By submitting your story, you'll join a network of individuals dedicated to exploring and sharing the mysteries of our world. Selected stories will remain the copyright of the original authors, and by participating, you'll be part of an anthology that stands against bullying and harassment, fostering a supportive and inclusive environment.

Don't miss this chance to have your voice heard and your experience shared. Submit your story today and become part of "Why We Are Supernatural." Help us unveil the mysteries that lie beyond our everyday reality and inspire others with your tale of the unexplained. Together, we can shed light on the shadows and understand why we are, indeed, supernatural. Learn more about how to take part by reading through this book!

Growing Up Haunted

The tale unfolds within the walls of my friend's family home, a residence they inhabited for many years.

The first chapter of this unsettling story is rooted in one of my friend's notorious birthday parties. Nestled in a quaint village in the Netherlands, this small town was the venue for the gathering, which drew not only the local teenagers but also a few from neighboring towns—myself included. During the festivities, I felt a pressing need to use the bathroom, which was located in the hallway.

This hallway, detached from the lively living room by a door, served as a passage to the bathroom and the stairs leading to the second floor. It was an area that felt isolated from the buzz of the party. After attending to my business, I encountered an inexplicable problem: the door simply refused to open. Despite my best efforts to turn the lock in every possible direction, the handle remained obstinately immobile. Panic set in as I struggled with the door for what felt like ten minutes. My distress was only alleviated when a relative of my friend arrived needing the bathroom; as if by some supernatural force, the door flew open just before they could knock, nearly colliding with them. I was drenched in relief and utterly exhausted. My friend and his family dismissed the incident as a mere malfunction, but the experience left me unsettled.

Years passed, and despite maintaining our friendship and frequently visiting his home, I harbored a lingering distrust of that bathroom, even as my friend and his relatives laughed off my unease.

Fast forward nearly three years to a warm spring day. I visited my friend once more, accompanied by two close friends. I had come under the pretense of needing to do homework, but I agreed to join them. I was in search of decent headphones, but he handed me a pair so worn and frayed they barely held together. Unable to concentrate downstairs due to the poor quality of the headphones, I decided to move my work to the upstairs sewing room, a decision I would soon regret.

The sewing room was a straightforward setup: a large table positioned against the north wall, with a clutter of clothes and other items hidden behind vaguely transparent sliding doors on the left. The room's atmosphere took a chilling turn as I attempted to focus on my homework. The temperature plummeted, prompting me to crank up the heating under the table. Although it offered brief respite, the cold persisted, gnawing at my concentration.

As I immersed myself in my work, an unsettling sensation grew stronger. I felt an unnerving presence, as though unseen eyes were watching me from behind the sliding doors. A particular dress hanging at waist height caught my attention, though I dared not look directly at it. The feeling of being observed intensified, and from the periphery of my vision, I glimpsed her—a spectral figure standing disturbingly close. Her presence was unmistakable; she did not want me there. Overcome by sheer terror, I shut my laptop and fled downstairs, my heart pounding with dread.

Upon bursting into the room where my friends were gathered, I recounted my experience. Their reactions ranged from skepticism to amusement, but the memory of our brief eye contact with the apparition remains vivid in my mind. Even now, as I recount the details, I can feel the phantom's gaze and the chill that accompanied it.

To this day, my friend dismisses my account with a laugh, but the haunting memories persist. As we've all grown older, I find solace in knowing that those visits to the house are a thing of the past.

A Hoarder's Haunting

I spent seventeen years living on a wetland, in a sprawling five-bedroom ranch house with a history as tangled as the marshlands surrounding it. The house, constructed in 1960, had been the sole residence of its original owner before my family moved in. The previous occupant, a man who had evidently filled the house with a lifetime's worth of hoarded possessions, had died in the hallway—a detail that would come to cast a long shadow over our experiences.

As a middle and high school student, I became acutely aware of the house's unsettling atmosphere. It began with subtle disturbances—footsteps echoing down the hallway in the dead of night and the erratic flickering of lights. Often, I would hear the lights clicking on and off with no apparent cause, as if some unseen hand were toying with the switches. These occurrences were disconcerting, but they were only the beginning of the house's eerie repertoire.

One evening, as I sat in the living room, the air around me grew unnervingly heavy. I was seated on the two-seater couch when I suddenly became aware of a presence. The sensation was unmistakable—a deep, rhythmic breathing right behind me, so close I could almost feel the warmth of it. I held my breath, straining to determine if the sound was my own. Glancing over at my two cats, who were perched atop the stand-up piano, I saw that they were watching me intently. The breathing persisted, and my cats' gaze was fixed on me, not on the unseen source of the sound.

Later, I shared my experience with my brother, only to discover that he had encountered the same unsettling phenomenon. He too had heard the heavy breathing, but from a different vantage point: lying on the four-seater couch at a different time. His description matched mine exactly— the same proximity, the same oppressive sound. It was as though the house had a particular fondness for that area behind the couch, a space charged with a lingering, malevolent energy.

But the breathing was just one facet of the house's dark side. There were many other unsettling occurrences that rendered our home a place of discomfort and unease. Objects seemed to move of their own accord, shadows flitted just beyond the edge of vision, and the silence of the house was frequently broken by inexplicable noises. Each corner of the house seemed to harbor its own secret, adding to the overall sense of dread that permeated our daily lives.

The most haunting aspect of living in

that house, however, was the relentless onslaught of nightmares. My sleep was plagued by vivid, terrifying dreams that left me shaken and exhausted. Each night brought a new horror, a continuation of the unsettling experiences I had while awake. The line between the waking world and the nightmares grew increasingly blurred, making it impossible to escape the house's grip, even in sleep.

Despite my family's attempts to brush off these experiences with practical explanations, the unease never truly dissipated. The house, with its storied past and unsettling occurrences, became a place I dreaded returning to after school. It wasn't merely a residence—it was a haunted shell of a home, burdened by its history and its restless former occupant.

Marked by Him

As a child, I experienced a series of chilling encounters that left an indelible mark on me, even before I fully understood what ghosts or demonic entities were. My first unsettling experience occurred when I was about five or six years old, in a government housing project in Ingleside, Texas. I often had vivid dreams where I was locked in a struggle over a toy with another child. Each time I awoke, a sense of dread would envelop me, a palpable cloud of impending doom that settled heavily over my body.

My mother would often leave my bedroom door open while she stayed up late, long after my brother and I were supposed to be asleep. My brother, just two or three years old, slept in a crib against one wall, while I was on the opposite side of the room in my bed. The only light in the room came from the flickering glow of the TV in the hallway, casting a dim and eerie light over our room. One night, I saw figures drifting into my bedroom in a misty, translucent form, moving in a line from the doorway, gliding between my brother's crib and my bed, and finally disappearing into the double closet doors. I could make out their facial features and the clothes they wore, but they seemed to float about six inches off the ground, with no visible feet. They never looked at us or acknowledged our presence. I remember crying out for my mother at the top of my lungs, and when she arrived, I asked her to shut the door because "the people keep coming into my room."

Though the dream about fighting over the toy seemed disconnected from the ghostly figures, I couldn't shake the feeling that the child in my dreams was somehow linked to the unsettling atmosphere of that place. The dream was always set in a pitch-black room with us quarreling over the toy, which felt just as frightening as the ghostly apparitions.

Several years later, when I was a little older, my family moved to another unit in the same complex, or perhaps my mother simply switched my brother's and my rooms. We had a new, large bed—a queen-sized mattress on a box spring—positioned against the wall. The room had a door on the left side and a closet on the right, about five feet from the bed. There was also a double window at the foot of our bed, about four feet away from the wall. During this time, my mother would come in for our nightly routine, tucking us in and leading us in a prayer, such as the Our Father.

One night, as we recited our prayer, I felt an overwhelming, inexplicable sensation that made me burst into uncontrollable laughter. My mother was deeply troubled and raised her voice, chastising me for laughing during our prayer and calling it "evil." She insisted that I finish the prayer with a serious demeanor, and we went to bed.

Later that night, I awoke to find the window glowing with yellow light from the street lamp outside, as usual. But this time, a dark silhouette of a creature was moving slowly past the window, disappearing into the darkness at the right side of the room. At the time, I had no understanding of demons or spirits, so I could only describe the creature as resembling the Count from Sesame Street —short and hunched over.

Years later, while watching a documentary about the Hat Man, a malevolent shadow figure, I was struck by a revelation. The documentary led me down a rabbit hole of online searches, where I found a drawing that matched precisely what I had seen as a child—a hunched creature moving across the window, illuminated by its glow. The discovery was mind-blowing, and though I didn't save the image, I have been unable to find it again.

"Something Grabbed Me!"

When I was about ten years old, my family followed a strict bedtime routine. All seven of us would tuck ourselves in, say our goodnights, and drift off to sleep at the same time. It was a ritual that gave us a sense of unity and comfort.

One night, just minutes after the lights had been extinguished and the house had settled into silence, I found myself needing to get up for one last trip to the bathroom. The house, a sprawling 2000 square foot structure, was dimly lit by the moonlight filtering through the windows. I navigated my way down the hallway, my hand trailing along the wall for guidance. As I approached the room on my right, I knew the bathroom was on the left.

I reached the bathroom door, but just as I was about to open it, something inexplicable happened. A large, powerful hand clamped around my right ankle with a force that felt both cold and muscular. It yanked me backward, dragging me across the hallway and into the center of a small, vacant bedroom. The terror I felt was overwhelming; I screamed at the top of my lungs, a scream that seemed to echo through the stillness of the house.

My parents, hearing my blood-curdling cry, rushed into the room to find out what was wrong. I was hysterical, barely able to form coherent words as I cried out, "Someone grabbed me!" My mom and stepdad quickly began to investigate, checking the locked windows and the closet, which had no access to an attic. Their concern was palpable as they searched for any logical explanation.

The only unusual feature of the room was a yin-yang symbol painted on the inside of the closet door. Beneath it was a grim note, a haunting message left by a previous occupant, detailing their struggles and despair. My mom had tried to scrub the symbol and note away when we first moved in, but the remnants were still faintly visible, like a ghost of the past clinging to the present.

Despite their thorough search, my parents found no physical evidence of an intruder or an explanation for the strange occurrence. The chilling feeling that had gripped me that night remained unexplained, leaving an unsettling mark on our otherwise ordinary home.

The Light Being

When I was between seven and nine years old, an unsettling encounter occurred that I've never quite been able to explain. I was lying in bed, facing the wall with the door positioned directly against it from the left side. As I struggled to fall asleep, something extraordinary happened.

A figure of light appeared as if materializing from the very door. It moved with purpose, crossing my room with a brisk pace before vanishing through the wall on my right. The figure was an ethereal shade of white or a very pale yellow. It didn't seem to wear clothes, but it wasn't exactly naked either—more like a human anatomy model, with its entire form glowing in a uniform color. It wasn't blindingly bright but had a gentle luminosity, akin to the glow of a high-brightness TV screen.

I was fully awake when this happened, as the sight was so startling that I immediately bolted out of bed and ran to my parents' room, my heart racing. I remember feeling a mix of fear and disbelief, urgently seeking comfort from them.

There was another incident that I recall vaguely, involving a blue figure. However, I believe this one was likely a nightmare, a product of the anxiety caused by the initial encounter. The details are hazy, and I remember almost nothing about it except the lingering unease it left behind.

To this day, I'm puzzled by the nature of these figures. I've never encountered a description of such entities in ghost lore or other accounts. If anyone knows what these figures might be or if they've experienced something similar, I'd be very interested to hear about it.

Grandma's Ghost Story

My grandmother has recounted a chilling story from her childhood more times than I can count, each telling leaving me with a lingering sense of unease.

When she and her sister were young, they lived in a modest house with their parents. On one eerie evening, they peered out of the window and spotted a man standing outside. He was dressed in a black suit and wore a hat that obscured his face.

The children were terrified and immediately told their mother about the mysterious figure. To their shock, their mother revealed that she had seen him too, though she offered no explanation for his presence.

The real horror, however, unfolded one night when the entire family was asleep. In the dead of night, while my grandmother and her siblings lay tucked in their beds, their mother saw the hat man again. This time, the figure was outside the house, and he moved in a disquieting manner. He appeared to float rather than walk, and most disturbingly, he had no feet—just empty voids where his legs should have been.

The hat man glided past the window and entered the house, moving with a slow, deliberate pace. My grandmother's mother watched in sheer terror as the figure floated through the house and came to a stop at the bottom of the staircase. An overwhelming sense of dread filled the room as she tried to call out, but no sound escaped her lips. It was as if her mouth had been sewn shut, rendering her mute and helpless. Despite her desperate attempts, she couldn't utter a single word or scream.

Paralyzed by fear, she could only watch as the hat man slowly ascended the stairs towards where the children were sleeping. Each step he took was measured and deliberate, heightening the suspense of what might happen next. Her inability to act or even make a sound only compounded her terror.

As the hat man made his way up the stairs, the oppressive silence seemed to stretch on forever. The weight of the unseen threat loomed heavy in the air. My grandmother's mother remained in her paralyzed state, her heart pounding in her chest, until the figure finally disappeared from view.

In the aftermath, my grandmother and her siblings awoke the next morning to find nothing amiss, but the memory of that night left a lasting scar. The story of the Hat Man became a haunting reminder of the unknown and the supernatural, one that continues to unsettle all who hear it.

Arizona Heat

In the sweltering summer of 2008, we found ourselves exploring the outskirts of a once desolate area in Arizona, near an old jail. Back then, the landscape was mostly barren desert, with only the beginnings of residential development. We were a group of friends hanging out in a cul-de-sac, enjoying the freedom that such an isolated place offered.

As dusk fell, I decided to jump out of a

truck we had been using. I was momentarily alone, away from the rest of the group, when something extraordinary happened. I glanced to my right, following an instinct that felt almost like guidance from my spiritual guides. What I saw froze me in place—a towering figure that stood between 8 and 10 feet tall, with menacing horns jutting forward from its head.

The entity's face and torso were obscured by shadows, leaving only its formidable legs visible. The legs resembled those of a horse, and its feet ended in cloven hooves. Most disturbing of all, it appeared to be hovering rather than walking, gliding towards me with an eerie, deliberate pace. The sheer presence of the being was enough to paralyze me with fear.

My friend, who was still in the truck, noticed my distress and yelled for me to get back inside. I scrambled, too terrified to think straight. I could barely muster the courage to drive, so my friend took control of the steering wheel while I stamped on the gas pedal. With the truck roaring to life, we sped away from the desolate stretch of road, leaving the haunting figure behind.

Years later, I sought the help of a medicine man to cleanse myself of lingering spiritual disturbances. During the cleansing, he confirmed a peculiar sensation I had felt—one that seemed to involve my spirit leaving my body. The night before this cleansing, I had seen a coyote, which seemed significant given my recent experiences. In my dreams, I had encountered both a coyote and a javelina, suggesting a deeper connection to Native traditions and symbols.

Reflecting on that night, I wonder if the encounter with the towering entity was a warning—a form of protection from something or someone that might have been a threat. The being's presence felt like a message to distance myself from the situation I was in and, possibly, from the people I was with at that time. While I managed to escape unscathed, the encounter left a lasting impression.

This experience serves as a reminder of the mysterious forces that might guide or protect us, even when we don't fully understand their intentions. It's crucial to approach such phenomena with caution and respect, recognizing that these encounters may carry significant meaning. For anyone seeking out these kinds of experiences, be mindful—such entities are not to be trifled with, and their appearances are not always as benign as they might seem.

Shroomed Up for Spirit

One dark and restless night, my friend—let's call him B—found himself in a fragile state of mind, deeply troubled and searching for answers. He had decided to take mushrooms, hoping to escape his mental anguish, but what he encountered was far beyond what he anticipated.

B had been playing with a Ouija board, a tool he had approached with skepticism, yet tonight he felt drawn to it with an inexplicable urgency. As the board began to move, he established contact with his best friend, K, who had tragically died in a car accident years earlier. B had been in the passenger seat that fateful night, the sole survivor of the crash that claimed K's life.

As B and I exchanged messages, he described an intense and unsettling sensation. He felt K's presence in the room, so palpable that he was convinced it was truly his late friend. K's spirit, he said, was filled with resentment and hate, conveying nothing but a cold, hostile energy. Despite the animosity, K's presence remained lingering, hauntingly tangible.

I advised B to confront the spirit, to express everything he had wished to say to K, and to encourage him to move on and find peace. B took this advice to heart, but the response I received from him was chilling. After a long, tense silence of more than fifteen minutes, B's message was disquieting: he described a profound, unsettling feeling—one he could only describe as "death crawling inside him."

He was unable to articulate the experience clearly, and as I probed for details, B revealed that the encounter had profoundly shaken him. He described an almost physical encounter with K's spirit—one that led him to pass out, not as one drifts into sleep, but as if he had fallen into an abyss. Before losing consciousness, B recounted K's haunting words: "I see the black in you." And then, the presence was gone.

When B awoke, he felt a deep, nauseating sickness inside him—a sense of dread and malaise that defied conventional explanations. He looked into a mirror and saw a reflection that confirmed his worst fears: he looked ill, but not with a typical flu or physical ailment. There was something dark and unsettling about his appearance that he couldn't quite understand.

This encounter leaves me grappling with profound questions. What does it mean when someone says "death crawls inside you"?

What could K's declaration, "I see the black in you," signify? Is there a deeper, more sinister meaning to these words and experiences?

While I am aware that B's altered state of mind may have influenced his perception, the intensity of his experience suggests something more profound. The Ouija board, often associated with opening doors to the unknown, might have indeed allowed something to cross over—a haunting presence that exploited B's vulnerability.

For those who dismiss this as mere drug-induced hallucination, I ask you to consider the weight of B's experience and the possible implications of communicating with the spirit world. There may be more to this encounter than meets the eye, and understanding it could require delving deeper into the realms of the supernatural.

Eerie Street

Prepare yourself for a journey through a series of unsettling experiences that have haunted me since childhood. Each location, each story, reveals a piece of a greater, chilling puzzle.

The Wausau Haunting

In 1970, when I was in third grade, my family relocated to Wausau, Wisconsin for six months due to my father's job. Our new home seemed ordinary at first, but strange occurrences soon began to unsettle me. Objects would shift on their own, and whispers echoed through the walls of my room. My parents dismissed these disturbances as figments of my overactive imagination, even going so far as to ban my favorite TV show, *Night Gallery*. It wasn't until thirty years later that my mother revealed a chilling truth: someone had died in my room.

Echoes in Appleton

After our stint in Wausau, we returned to Appleton, moving into a house with a problematic landlady. It felt surreal to be back at Sacred Heart School, as if time had folded on itself. The sense of déjà vu deepened when we relocated once more in 1972. The small ranch house quickly became too cramped for our family of six. My sister, Amy, reported seeing a shadowy figure in the basement, and eerie sounds of footsteps ascending the stairs at night plagued us. The basement itself became a source of dread, confirmed years later when my parents disclosed that someone had committed suicide there.

Enigmatic Residence on E Frances

In 1973, we moved down the block to E Frances, a house with its own dark history. My parents occupied the downstairs bedroom, while the three bedrooms upstairs seemed to harbor an unsettling presence. My brother's room was persistently colder than the rest, and I was plagued by disturbing dreams about a boy who supposedly lived in the attic, lurking in my closet. I also felt eyes on me when playing in my father's workshop, where lights would flicker unpredictably.

Our attempts to navigate this eerie environment often led to frightening experiences. We kids would race downstairs to fetch items, only to feel as if we were being chased. Cupboard doors would slam shut on their own, and objects would move mysteriously. My sister Sarah reported seeing a little girl with glowing red eyes, both by her bed and near the downstairs closet. We remained in this house until 1978, with the paranormal activity never fully abating.

The Reno Condo

Years later, while living with two roommates in a condo in Reno, I knew something was off from the beginning. My silky terrier, Ziggy, often whimpered and growled at unseen forces in the middle of the night. Footsteps echoed up and down the stairs, adding to the sense of unease. My roommate John, who was keen to impress women with free tickets to my stage hypnotist show, paid little heed to the strange occurrences. However, things took a turn when John's friend Dominic experienced something terrifying in my room.

Dominic had heard strange noises and demanded that the spirit reveal itself. He captured a disturbing photograph of what appeared to be an apparition. When our ghost-hunting efforts were validated by three separate ghostbusters, they reported encounters with both a young boy and girl who seemed to take a liking to my dog, as well as a darker presence known as the "Dark Man." Terri Landry from the news brought her Ghost Hunter's Team, who confirmed these findings and added their own chilling accounts.

Haunting at Cheryl and Dave's

Not all of my ghostly experiences occurred in my own homes. During a visit to friends Cheryl and Dave in Pittsburgh, where I was in a long-distance relationship with a psychic woman, we encountered another ghostly phenomenon. After dinner, their dogs barked furiously, and the parrot squawked incessantly. Cheryl revealed that these disturbances were the work of their resident ghosts. Our investigation yielded fascinating EVPs and photographs of orbs. Upon returning home, my psychic partner and I felt an overwhelming sense that a spirit had followed us. This eerie sensation, which I had only felt once before, led us to believe that the ghost had, in some way, safeguarded my house from further disturbances.

These experiences span years and locations, each contributing to a tapestry of supernatural encounters that continue to haunt me. Whether the entities were warnings, manifestations of unresolved pasts, or something else entirely, they have left an indelible mark on my life.

The Girls in the Night

It began with a vivid dream that seemed to blur the lines between reality and something far more sinister. In this dream, I found myself walking alone down a desolate, shadowy street. The only beacon of light in the oppressive darkness was a store, its flickering sign promising refuge. As I approached, I became aware of a presence behind me—a girl in a red dress, trailing silently but menacingly.

Inside the store, the red-dressed girl remained outside, her form barely visible through the glass doors. It was then that another girl, this one in a white dress, appeared. She seemed to skip towards me with an aura of warmth and reassurance. Without a word, she took my hand and guided me towards the exit. I felt a chill as I confided in her, "The girl in red wants me dead. That's what I feel."

The girl in white simply smiled and led me out of the store. As expected, the girl in red followed us at a distance, her presence a dark shadow on the periphery. The girl in white turned to face the red-dressed specter and, with a voice filled with authority and defiance, shouted, "She is not yours!" As she spoke, the girl in red vanished into thin air. I awoke shortly thereafter, heart racing and sweat cooling on my brow.

Weeks passed, and the dream slipped from my memory. One evening, while chatting with friends and lounging in bed, an uneasy feeling crept over me. I dismissed it, attributing it to nothing more than the usual discomfort. However, as I turned to settle more comfortably, my blood ran cold. Standing there, in the dimly lit corner of my room, was the very girl from my dream—clad in that haunting red dress. Before I could react, she vanished into the air as if she had never been there.

Since that night, an unsettling sense of being watched has clung to me. It feels as though an invisible presence is constantly near, observing, waiting. It's a chilling reminder of that dream, and I can't shake the feeling that I am somehow marked for something beyond my understanding.

Echoes of the Haunted House

For more than half of my life, addiction has been a dark shadow looming over me. In the throes of one harrowing episode, I encountered something that defied all reason. It was in 2009, when I was just fifteen, that I faced a night of terror that still haunts me.

Desperate and overwhelmed, I had decided to take a drastic measure. I consumed an entire bottle of phentermine, a decision that would plunge me into a world beyond comprehension. About an hour after ingesting the pills, my heart began to race uncontrollably. Paranoia gripped me like a vice, and I bolted from my bed, only to find a dark, shadowy figure lurking in the corner of my room. The fear that coursed through me was paralyzing, rendering me silent and immobile. In a frantic attempt to escape, I dashed into the kitchen, my mind racing with dread.

As I stumbled down the hall, my terror intensified. I started to hallucinate hands emerging from doorways, beckoning me with eerie waves. Each time I approached, the hands vanished, leaving me more disoriented and frightened. Dark figures seemed to crawl through the house, only to disappear the moment I got close. It felt as though some malevolent force was toying with me, escalating my sense of dread.

The most unsettling vision of that night was a figure at the end of the hall—a witch doctor-like entity with pale white paint and a loincloth. It looked like a spectral boy, and as he called out to me, I felt an inexplicable urge to confront him. As I drew nearer, the figure faded away, reminiscent of a scene from *Hereditary* where the protagonist sees her mother in the dark. The sight left me puzzled and shaken, unable to discern reality from hallucination.

The terror did not end with that night. Exhausted and frazzled, I went to school the next day, trying to act normal despite the lingering effects of the drugs. All day, I heard voices calling my name, and when I asked my peers about it, they looked at me as if I were out of my mind.

While it's easy to dismiss my experience as a drug-induced trip, there is more to the story. Other members of my family have experienced strange phenomena in that house. From 1994 to 2010, my mom, my uncle, and my cousin all reported encounters with sleep paralysis. Our home was a revolving door for family members, and many others might have had their own experiences.

This wasn't my first brush with the supernatural in that house. Before we moved out, I often felt the sensation of children running around me on the tile floors, even though I was home alone. My cousin and I also witnessed one of my grandmother's porcelain dolls move on its own. My grandmother, though Americanized, maintained some traditional Hispanic practices, lighting candles and performing rituals for her family's prosperity. I sometimes wonder if these rituals disturbed something unseen or if the house itself harbored a dark history.

Whatever the cause, the echoes of that haunted house have left an indelible mark on my psyche, a chilling reminder of the shadows that linger just beyond the veil of our understanding.

The Shadow at the Top of the Stairs

My unsettling experiences began when I was about eight years old. My family and I had lived in the same house since I was two, and it seemed like any ordinary home. The layout was simple: when you turned the corner to head up the stairs, the first thing you saw was my room, next to it was my brother's, and behind the wall at the top of the stairs was my dad's room.

From the moment I could remember, a shadowy, man-shaped figure would appear at the top of the stairs whenever I walked down. It was always in the corner of my eye, just on the edge of my vision. At first, I dismissed it as paranoia—after all, I was home alone often, the nights were dark, and my brother's room, which was always closed and shrouded in shadows, only added to my anxiety. My fascination with ghost adventures on YouTube didn't help either. Yet, this figure persisted, even when the lights were on in the hallway and my brother's room.

The shadowy figure would loom at the top of the stairs, seemingly emerging from my brother's room. Every time I tried to fully turn and face it, the figure vanished. I was convinced it was a figment of my imagination, spurred by my fears and the dark corners of the house.

Eventually, I confided in my dad about the eerie sightings. To my surprise, he revealed that before I was born, he and my uncle had played with a Ouija board in my brother's room. At the time, I didn't believe much in the supernatural, including Ouija boards, and my dad had never given me details about their experience. He said it was something he decided to keep from me because I was "so young," and to this day, he refuses to elaborate further.

Despite my dad's attempts to dismiss my fears, the shadowy figure continued to haunt me. Each time I'd see it, I'd stand frozen, staring at it out of the corner of my eye, only for it to disappear the moment I turned my head.

As the years have passed, I've wondered if I'm merely imagining the shadow or if there's something more to it. Could Ouija boards truly summon such figures, or am I simply seeing what I want to see, influenced by childhood fears and lingering memories? The shadow at the top of the stairs remains a chilling reminder of something unseen, a mystery that lingers in the dark corners of my mind.

The Shadows of the Cardiff Catacombs

I spent three years working as an administrative and clerical officer in the Radiology department of a large hospital in Cardiff, Wales. During that time, I witnessed a myriad of unsettling events—from patients dying during MRI scans to the bizarre cases like one where a patient needed an X-ray to investigate a rather disturbing insertion. Yet, it was the nights that proved to be the most unnerving.

The night shifts began at 7:00 PM and lasted until 8:30 AM. We typically worked three consecutive nights before getting four days off. By the third night, exhaustion was a constant companion. However, this particular night was the first of the three, so fatigue was not yet a factor.

The shift had begun ordinarily. I took over from the day staff, logged into my computer, and set up my phone to watch the latest series on Netflix. Radiology nights were usually marked by downtime, providing ample opportunity to catch up on shows or movies.

The first few hours were uneventful, but as my break approached, I decided to venture to the hospital's Sanctuary—a multi-faith chapel located on the 5th floor. This chapel was a rare refuge of tranquility amidst the hospital's chaos, but getting there required a journey through the hospital's eerie tunnels.

The hospital, being the largest in Wales and a teaching facility, was also quite old. Its labyrinthine tunnels—dimly lit corridors, abandoned rooms, and decrepit areas—were notorious among the staff. These catacombs included the morgue and had earned a reputation for being unsettling. Whispers of apparitions in old-fashioned uniforms and strange shadows often circulated among the staff, though I had never been particularly affected by these tales.

On this particular night, I set off through the tunnels, my key card granting me access. The tunnels were as dark and foreboding as ever. I walked briskly, trying to ignore the creeping sensation that someone was following me. The sound of heavy breathing echoed behind me, making me pause and turn. Yet, when I looked, there was nothing there—just the muted hum of old pipes and distant machinery.

The sensation of being watched grew more intense. I tried to brush off my unease but soon found myself in an unfamiliar section of the tunnels, filled with old, abandoned hospital equipment—stretchers, beds, and outdated machinery left to rot in the darkness. The air was thick with dust, and the stench of decay permeated the space. My sense of direction faltered; the once-familiar corridors seemed to stretch endlessly in every direction.

Panic began to set in. My chest tightened, and I struggled to breathe. I clutched at my chest and sprinted down the winding corridors, desperately seeking a sign or exit. The feeling of being observed was now overwhelming. Suddenly, I was struck with a forceful impact on my arm, as if someone had swung a heavy object at me. I collapsed, crawling along the cold, dusty floor, my heart racing.

Then, I saw it—a black mist with glowing red eyes hovering about twenty meters away in the corridor. The sight was both mesmerizing and terrifying. Was this the entity that had been following me? I didn't wait to find out. Fueled by adrenaline, I ran through what felt like a maze of endless corridors until I finally encountered a housekeeper (janitor). He noticed my pale face and inquired about my distress.

Before I could explain, he grabbed my arms firmly and asked, "Did you see it too?" His words sent chills down my spine. I could only nod, unable to articulate my fear.

That night marked the end of my explorations in the tunnels. To this day, I hear murmurs about strange occurrences in those underground passages. What exactly I saw that night remains a mystery. Was it a figment of my imagination, a result of stress and exhaustion, or something more sinister? The janitor's question—"Did you see it too?"— haunted me, leaving me with more questions than answers. One thing I know for certain: I have no intention of uncovering the truth behind whatever lurks in those shadowy depths.

Guardian at the Cradle

I've always considered myself a practical person, someone who relies on logic and evidence. Ghosts and the supernatural were never part of my reality—until that cold November night when everything changed.

Tom and I had recently moved into a charming old Victorian house on the outskirts of town. I loved the place for its character and history, but Tom was more skeptical. Despite his reservations, we settled in, and soon, our lives were blessed with the arrival of our daughter, Lily.

Life with a newborn was exhausting. Lily had trouble sleeping, and the endless nights of crying left me feeling frazzled and sleep-deprived. Tom worked late often, and one night, when Lily was just three months old, I was alone in the nursery, desperately trying to calm her.

The room was dimly lit by a single lamp, and I was rocking Lily in the antique cradle that had been Tom's grandmother's. I had always thought of it as just a beautiful piece of furniture, but that night, it seemed to hold a deeper significance. As I struggled to soothe Lily's cries, I felt an unsettling chill creep into the room. The air grew heavy, and I shivered despite the warmth.

Then, a soft, melodic lullaby began to fill the room. It was an old tune, one I didn't recognize. The melody was gentle, almost ethereal, and it seemed to resonate through the room, easing my frayed nerves. I looked around, puzzled by the unexpected sound.

That's when I saw him. At first, I could hardly believe my eyes—a man standing near the cradle. He was dressed in vintage clothing, like something from another era: a long, dark coat and a cravat. His presence was calm and soothing, and despite my fear, I felt a strange sense of comfort.

The man didn't speak but gazed at Lily with a protective look. He slowly began to rock the cradle, and the lullaby continued to play softly. Lily's cries diminished, replaced by peaceful coos. I stood there, my skepticism momentarily suspended, as the figure's presence seemed to bring a serene calm to the room.

The man stayed for only a few moments before gradually fading away. As he disappeared, the room's temperature returned to normal, and Lily fell into a deep, tranquil sleep. I stood there, dumbfounded, my mind racing to process what had just happened.

When Tom got home, I told him everything. He listened, though I could tell he was skeptical. He attributed it to exhaustion and stress. But for me, the experience was undeniable. The next day, I decided to investigate further.

I visited the local historian to learn more about the house. To my amazement, I discovered that the previous owner was Edward Caldwell, a well-respected community figure known for his kindness and work with children. Edward had been deeply involved in children's charities and was known for his soothing presence, especially with infants.

It was then that everything fell into place. The lullaby, the comforting figure, the sense of peace—it all made sense. Edward Caldwell had been a guardian angel for my daughter during a time of need. Though my rational mind still questioned the supernatural, I couldn't deny the profound impact of that night.

To this day, I remember that November evening with a mixture of awe and gratitude. I may never fully understand the hows or whys of that experience, but I've come to accept that some mysteries are beyond our comprehension. What I do know is that a gentle spirit, once a guardian in life, had watched over my daughter, and that knowledge is a comfort I carry with me always.

Midnight Shadow

Last night—or rather, early this morning—something happened that I can't easily explain. It was precisely 3:33 AM, a time I had never given much thought to until now. I was lounging on my couch, lost in thought and scrolling through my phone, when I noticed something peculiar out of the corner of my eye.

At first, it was just a fleeting movement—a dark, shadowy figure crouched and moving past my bedroom door. It was an indistinct shape, neither clearly human nor entirely formless. As soon as I turned to look directly at it, the figure vanished. My heart pounded in my chest, and a cold sweat broke out across my forehead. I felt a bone-deep fear and the unnerving sensation that I was being watched.

I've lived in this house for 11 years, and this was the first time I'd ever experienced anything like this. The only other unusual occurrence I could recall was from about six years ago when I heard knocking sounds. In a curious, perhaps misguided, attempt to communicate, I began tapping out patterns on the walls, only to have the knocking sounds mimic my own rhythms in return. It was strange, but nothing compared to the shadow I had just seen.

The fear and confusion left me paralyzed on the couch. I scanned the room, trying to find some rational explanation, but the darkness was still and silent. My thoughts raced as I considered the possibility of stress-induced hallucinations. I've been under a significant amount of stress lately, dealing with numerous personal challenges that have left me on edge.

Driven by a need for answers, I decided to do some research. It turns out that stress and anxiety can indeed contribute to experiences like seeing shadowy figures. It made sense in some ways, given my current state of mind. But even with this explanation, I couldn't shake the feeling of dread that had settled over me.

As I write this, I still grapple with the experience. Was it a trick of the mind, a result of overwhelming stress, or something more sinister? The fear remains palpable, and although I hope it was just a fleeting illusion brought on by my anxious state, the sight of that shadowy figure has left an indelible mark on my sense of security in my own home.

Apparitions of Our Home

Hauntings are no stranger to my life or my home. From childhood through to the present, my experiences with the supernatural have been countless and unsettling. Yet recently, the disturbances have taken on a new, more menacing tone.

It began with small, disquieting occurrences: my medications disappearing from their usual places, photographs inexplicably falling from their frames, and the occasional flicker of lights or the creaking open of heavy drawers in the dead of night. At first, I tried to brush these off as coincidences or simple misplacement. But as time went on, the incidents grew more frequent and alarming.

My mother has a penchant for collecting occult artifacts, and I began to worry that these spirits, drawn by her collection, had become unnervingly attached to me. Their presence was no longer benign; it had become both mischievous and aggressive.

One evening, as I sat in the dimly lit living room, I heard voices that seemed to mimic those of my family members. These voices called my name with eerie precision, their tones indistinguishable from those of my loved ones. Yet, when I turned to confront them, there was no one there. The air grew cold, and shadows seemed to shift with a sinister purpose.

The apparitions themselves were more than just fleeting glimpses. Full-blown figures would materialize, standing motionless in my line of sight. They remained unresponsive to the hustle and bustle of daily life, only acknowledging their surroundings when someone ventured too close. Their presence was disquieting; they seemed to exist in a realm apart from our own.

These manifestations did more than merely unsettle me—they started to invade my dreams. Nightmares plagued my sleep, often featuring these spectral figures, leaving me with a lingering sense of dread that persisted throughout the day. Despite their disturbing nature, these entities had not inflicted physical harm upon me. Still, the psychological toll was immense.

I couldn't shake the feeling that something had changed. These spirits, once perhaps harmless or indifferent, had taken a personal interest in my life. The sense of being watched, the intrusive voices, and the silent, menacing figures were a constant reminder of their presence. I remained uncertain whether they were truly malevolent or merely playing cruel games with my sanity.

What was clear, however, was that my home, once a sanctuary, had become a battleground between the living and the restless dead.

Hauntings of Ambergate Pumping Station

In the summer of 2008, I was working as a contractor and Control Systems Engineer for Severn Trent Water. My duties took me to Ambergate Pumping Station, situated next to Carsington Water in Derbyshire, England. It was a grand Victorian structure, imposing and labyrinthine, extending three storeys below ground.

One late afternoon, around 4 p.m., I was

summoned to the pumping station. I was swamped with work, so I inquired why one of the operators couldn't handle it instead. Someone chuckled and said, "Oh, it's haunted. Sausage won't go near it." Sausage, one of the operators, had a reputation for avoiding the station, but I dismissed it as a joke. I've always been open to the idea of ghosts, having experienced the occasional odd occurrence, but nothing particularly unsettling—until that day.

Experience One: The Toolbag Incident

Descending the three flights of metal stairs with my small bag of tools and a folding table, I entered the cold, damp darkness of the pump house. Despite the summer heat outside, the interior was frigid and poorly lit, the air heavy with the smell of rust and decay.

The task was straightforward: test a panel and trace a fault. I had just settled in when my toolbag—heavy with spanners, screwdrivers, and other essentials—suddenly flew off the table. It soared six feet across the room, hitting the wall with a resounding thud and scattering its contents onto the floor. I didn't witness the incident, but the sound was unmistakable. I spun around, bewildered. There was no one else in the room, and the bag had not been precariously balanced. It would have taken a deliberate force to propel it that distance.

I gathered my tools, placed them back in the bag, and set it on the table once more. The rest of the job went without incident, and I quickly finished up. When I returned to the Severn Trent offices, one of the guys jokingly asked, "Have fun in there, Neil?" I just nodded, choosing not to elaborate on the unsettling experience.

Experience Two: The Flickering Lights

Two weeks later, I was called back to Ambergate. The experience that day was even stranger. I arrived around midday, carrying my tools and metal table, and switched on the lights before descending the stairs. As soon as I reached the bottom, the lights went out, plunging me into pitch darkness.

I groped my way back up the stairs, feeling increasingly uneasy. I managed to find the light switch and turned it on. But as I descended once more, the lights flicked off again as soon as I reached the bottom. The growing sense of dread was palpable.

Determined to find a solution, I retrieved some duct tape from my car and taped it over the light switch. When I returned to the basement, the lights began flickering violently. It was as if someone—or something—was playing with the switch, unable to turn it off completely. The incessant clicking of the switch echoed through the empty halls.

I stayed there for about 10 to 15 minutes, enduring the flickering lights and eerie clicking sounds. The atmosphere was oppressive, and I could feel a chill in the air. I completed my task as quickly as possible and left the station, my nerves frayed.

Aftermath and Reflections

I shared my experiences with a few people, but the explanations offered were unsatisfactory. One suggested I must have placed the toolbag too close to the edge of the table, though this did not account for its distance from where it fell. Another proposed a colleague might have been playing a prank, but this seemed improbable. The station was remote, and the effort required to follow me and execute such a detailed prank seemed excessive.

To this day, I have not returned to Ambergate Pumping Station, and I have no desire to. The unexplained events, combined with the eerie atmosphere of the place, have left a lasting impression on me. The haunting presence I encountered there remains a mystery, and I am content to leave it undisturbed.

The Moving Sign

It was a crisp autumn afternoon in the Seattle Metro area, specifically in downtown Redmond. My girlfriend and I had just checked into a hotel and decided to walk to a nearby shopping and restaurant center. The streets were bustling with activity—road construction was in full swing, and the air was filled with the clatter of machinery and the murmur of workers in hard hats.

As we approached an intersection, I

noticed something peculiar. A large "Road Closed" sign, wide enough to block an entire lane, shifted unexpectedly. It moved over a foot on one end, as if an unseen force had nudged it. My girlfriend, engrossed in our conversation, didn't see it. I paused, staring at the sign as it settled back into place, and then glanced around the street, trying to make sense of what I'd just witnessed.

"What's up?" my girlfriend asked, noticing my sudden stop.

"That sign just moved by itself," I said, pointing. "It's at least 75 pounds, and it shifted over a foot. I don't know how that happened."

My girlfriend shrugged it off, and we continued to the shopping center, though I couldn't shake the feeling of unease.

The following day, we were waiting in the hotel lobby for our ride to Sea-Tac Airport. As we read through our phones, I brought up the strange incident again. My girlfriend, who was quite religious, looked uneasy and suggested we shouldn't discuss such things—it was better to ignore them.

Curious and unsettled, I decided to investigate further. Despite my girlfriend's reluctance, I walked back to the intersection, two blocks away from the hotel. The road was quiet, with only a construction worker nearby, seemingly lost in his phone.

I approached the sign, which was still in place, and gave it a push. It was indeed as heavy as I had remembered, confirming that moving it would have required significant force. The construction worker barely glanced up, absorbed in his own world.

My girlfriend later insisted it must have been the wind that caused the sign to move. Yet, the day was eerily calm—there was no breeze to speak of.

I couldn't help but wonder: What force

had moved that sign? Why had I seen it shift when no one else seemed to notice? My late mother had often spoken of ghostly encounters, and I had experienced a few myself as a child. Was this another sign of something beyond the ordinary?

Pact with Lilith

I don't even know where to begin with this story. It's one of those experiences that leaves you questioning reality and wondering if you're alone in this strange world.

My relationship with Lilith has always been intricately tied to my sexuality. It started with a pact I made with her, a decision to seal my fertility. To my astonishment, it worked—without a shadow of a doubt.

After making the pact, Lilith became a constant presence in my sexual life. She seemed to shield me from unwanted pregnancies, STDs, and bad sexual experiences. More than that, she became a guiding force in building my confidence, especially in the realm of pleasure. She constantly urged me to embrace my desires fully, no matter how they manifested.

During my solitary rituals of self-discovery, which I often referred to as "Me Time," Lilith would sometimes appear. I didn't think much of it at first. My imagination has always been vivid, and visualization comes naturally to me. But over time, I noticed a dramatic shift in my experiences. Where I once had a lackluster sex life, I now found myself intensely aroused, my orgasms reaching new, almost magical heights. The sensations were so electrifying, it felt as though live electricity was coursing through me.

Just recently, during one of my regular "Me Time" sessions, something extraordinary happened. As I was reaching the peak of pleasure, I closed my eyes and there she was —Lilith, standing beside me. Her presence was unmistakable, her excitement palpable. She placed her hand gently beneath my stomach, her face lit up with pride and anticipation. She urged me to finish, her energy mingling with mine.

In that moment, the intensity of my orgasm skyrocketed. It was an overwhelming surge of energy, causing me to arch my back, gaze fixed on the ceiling, and my body shaking uncontrollably. The experience was so powerful, so otherworldly, that it left me reeling.

I am still in shock, trying to make sense of what happened. Just the night before, I had shared with others how Lilith influenced my sex life, and now it felt like she had confirmed my experiences in a dramatic way.

Connection with the Unknown

It all began when I decided to reach out to Lord Lucifer for the first time. Driven by a deep curiosity and a desire to understand more about the otherworldly, I composed a heartfelt letter. I carefully crafted my offering, set up a candle, and turned to my tarot cards for divination. The process was solemn and deliberate, a blend of reverence and wonder.

As I completed the ritual, a profound sense of peace enveloped me. It was as though Lord Lucifer's presence was a gentle, reassuring embrace. The atmosphere was calm, and I felt a safe, almost comforting energy surrounding me. It was a feeling that lingered long after the ritual had ended.

Days passed, and I started to notice something unusual. While I was going about my daily routines, I began hearing voices. They weren't loud or intrusive; rather, they seemed to come from nowhere and were often accompanied by a sudden sense of clarity. It was as if someone was gently interjecting their thoughts into my own.

One instance stands out vividly. I had a pounding headache, a nagging discomfort that made it difficult to concentrate. As I reached for the Tylenol bottle, a voice spoke softly in my ear, "You really should be drinking more water, darling. You're awfully dehydrated, and that's why your head hurts." The voice was calm, soothing, and carried a warmth that felt oddly familiar. I paused, puzzled, and took a sip of water. The headache gradually eased, confirming the voice's advice.

The more this phenomenon occurred, the more I pondered its source. Was I merely talking to myself, my mind weaving these comments as a form of self-advice? Or could it be that Lord Lucifer, or perhaps another spirit, was communicating with me? My experiences with clairaudience have always been present, but this was different—more direct and personal.

I questioned my own sanity, wondering if my mind was simply playing tricks on me. Yet, the consistency of the voice and the relevance of its messages left me intrigued. Was this a manifestation of Lord Lucifer's presence, offering guidance and support? Or was I losing touch with reality, confounding my inner thoughts with external voices?

In the quiet moments of reflection, I mulled over these encounters, unsure of their meaning but deeply aware of their impact. The voice, whether a manifestation of my own psyche or a genuine connection with the otherworldly, had a profound effect on me. It reminded me that the boundaries between our inner selves and the unseen world are often more porous than we realize.

As I continued my journey, I remained open to these experiences, embracing the mystery while seeking clarity. The voices persisted, gentle and guiding, leaving me to navigate the delicate line between the known and the unknown.

Pawn Shop Haunting

I've been running the pawn shop on Elm Street for over fifteen years. It's an ordinary place, filled with old watches, dusty furniture, and the occasional oddity that slips through the cracks. But nothing prepared me for what happened last month.

It all started with a peculiar item—a vintage mirror, ornately framed and covered in a layer of grime that hinted at decades of neglect. It was a quiet Wednesday when a disheveled man came in, practically begging me to buy it. He claimed it was an heirloom that had been passed down through his family, but he needed quick cash and was willing to part with it for a song. I took the mirror, paid him, and thought nothing more of it. It looked like it could fetch a good price, and that was enough for me.

The first sign that something was wrong came two nights later. I was closing up shop when I heard a loud crash coming from the back room. I rushed to see what had happened and found the mirror on the floor, its glass shattered. I figured it was just an accident—maybe an unstable shelf or a gust of wind. I cleaned up the mess and went home, but the uneasy feeling wouldn't leave me.

Over the next few days, things took a turn for the worse. Objects began moving on their own—small trinkets and coins would appear in different places than where I had left them. The lights flickered uncontrollably, and a chilling draft seemed to follow me through the shop. I dismissed it as stress or a series of unfortunate coincidences until the night the noises began.

It was the dead of night when I was jolted awake by a loud, guttural growl echoing through the shop. My heart raced as I lay in bed, trying to convince myself it was just a bad dream. But then, I heard it again—closer this time. A shuffling sound, as though something was dragging itself across the floor. The growling grew louder, more insistent, and I knew I had to do something.

The following morning, I contacted a local paranormal investigator who came highly recommended. He was a friend of my son's, someone they called Dakota, known as the Specialist of the Strange. When I told him what was happening, he listened intently, his face growing serious.

He agreed to come by and take a look at the mirror. When he arrived, Dakota was thorough in his examination. He walked through the shop, noting the disturbances, and then he approached the mirror with a solemn expression. Without saying much, he wrapped it carefully and loaded it into his car.

The change was almost instantaneous. As soon as Dakota left with the mirror, the atmosphere in the shop shifted. The draft stopped, the lights stabilized, and the growling ceased. It was as though a heavy weight had been lifted. I didn't ask Dakota what he did with the mirror or where he took it—I didn't want to know. The sight of him handling it with such care was enough for me.

I was relieved beyond words when the shop returned to its normal state. I had no desire to revisit the nightmare I had just endured. I have no idea what Dakota did or how he managed to quell whatever dark presence was attached to that mirror. I'm not sure I even want to know. The less I know, the better.

Sometimes, when I'm alone in the shop, I think I hear whispers from the corner of the room, but I brush them off as my imagination running wild. All I know for sure is that the nightmare is over, and I've learned to be cautious about the items I take in. As for that mirror, I hope it's found a place far away from me—wherever it belongs, far from my life.

Shadows of Applachia

About two years ago, one of my friends was about to move from the Appalachian region to Florida, so we decided to go catfishing one last time before he left. We didn't catch a thing that night, but the thrill of being out on the river was enough. We packed up around 2 or 3 a.m., ready to head back home.

The drive was uneventful until we hit a thick fog. I remember having the window cracked open because I was smoking a stogie, and my friend was half-asleep in the passenger seat, but still alert enough to be aware. I had just glanced up from changing the song on my phone when I saw something that made my blood run cold.

Right in front of the car, illuminated by the headlights, was a figure I can only describe as a shadow being. It was enormous, standing on two legs, but it was nothing more than a dark, shapeless void against the night. There were no details, no features—just a black silhouette that seemed to absorb all light. It was as if a piece of darkness had taken on a human-like form.

The figure moved swiftly, crossing the road in front of us. My heart was pounding as I watched, paralyzed by a mix of fear and disbelief. As it passed, it brushed against the tall grass and weeds on the side of the road. The noise was deafening—like a freight train tearing through the foliage. The sound of the vegetation snapping and rustling was amplified by the quiet of the foggy night. The sheer speed and force of its movement sent a chill down my spine, making me shiver uncontrollably.

My friend and I didn't speak much during the drive home, both of us lost in our own thoughts. We exchanged a few words, confirming that we had indeed seen the same thing—a shadowy figure that defied any rational explanation. We joked about it to lighten the mood, but the experience left a mark on both of us. Neither of us had ever encountered anything like it before or since.

To this day, I can't shake the image of that shadow being or the eerie sound it made as it moved past us. If anyone has had a similar encounter or has insight into what we saw that night, I'd be very interested to hear your experiences.

Snowman of Calhoun County

Growing up in rural Calhoun County, West Virginia, my sister and I were accustomed to the isolation that came with living on land passed down through generations of my father's family. Our property was surrounded by dense woodlands, stretching for hundreds of acres, a vast and untamed wilderness that we were taught to respect and fear.

Our parents, despite their simplicity, were strict about their values. My father was a handyman with a knack for fixing anything, despite his lack of formal education. My mother preferred the quiet of our home and had little interest in traveling beyond the county lines. They emphasized the importance of succeeding in school and heeding their warnings about the dangers lurking in the woods surrounding our home.

Among the stories they shared, one stood out—the legend of the Snowman. According to my father, the Snowman was a fearsome spirit that resided in a hidden burial mound throughout most of the year. It would emerge with the first snowfall and prowl the area until the last frost. This creature was a remnant of a darker time, feared by the Mingo people who once inhabited the region in the early 1700s. My father recounted a horrific tale of a massacre of the Mingo people, after which the Snowman allegedly gathered the bodies and transported them to its hidden mound. The Snowman was described as a tall, rotund being covered in long white hair, with a face obscured entirely by its own cascading locks.

Our parents drilled into us the importance of staying indoors after dark, particularly during the winter months when the Snowman was said to be active. The house was kept eerily quiet during those times, a precaution against drawing the attention of this malevolent entity.

In January 1979, when my sister and I were in our early teens, an unsettling event occurred that confirmed the terrifying legend we had grown up with. One evening, around 8 p.m., we were huddled in the kitchen, diligently working on our homework. Our father had just walked in from the living room, grabbed his coat, and stepped out into the frigid night air. I asked my mother what he was doing, and she explained that he had forgotten to bring in the firewood.

Almost immediately after her reply, my father burst back through the door, looking pale and shaken. He grabbed one of the kitchen chairs and wedged it against the door. With trembling hands, he opened the cellar door, retrieved his 12-gauge shotgun, and grabbed a handful of pumpkin-ball shells. Confused and alarmed, I asked my mother what was happening. Her response was chilling: "The Snowman—he's out there."

Without hesitation, I ran upstairs to the attic, eager to catch a glimpse of whatever had disturbed my father. My sister followed closely behind. From the attic window, we watched the dark, fog-shrouded garden below. For what felt like an eternity, nothing moved. Then, my sister pointed to the garden, and my heart sank.

There, in the garden, stood the Snowman. It was enormous, easily eight feet tall, a towering figure that seemed to blend into the darkness. It moved with a slow, deliberate gait, standing upright before crouching down to dig into the frozen earth. The figure was a shadowy silhouette, its face completely obscured by the long, white hair that covered its entire body. The hair seemed to ripple and sway as it moved, but there were no discernible facial features.

After several minutes of this eerie ritual, the Snowman stood up and began to move closer to the house. Fear surged through me as I realized my father had been right all along. The creature turned and slowly retreated into the woods, disappearing into the shadows.

We never saw the Snowman again. The following days were marked by an unsettling silence, as if the entire world was holding its breath. My mother, who still lives in the old house, often speaks of hearing distant screams at night. She believes they are the restless spirits of the Mingo people, victims of the Snowman's dark past.

To this day, the memory of that night remains vivid. The Snowman is a legend that has taken on a new, terrifying reality for me, a reminder that some old tales are rooted in something far more sinister than mere folklore.

Visit from Gabriel

I've been meaning to share this story from back in 2006 when I was just 19 and pregnant with my now 10-year-old daughter.

I was staying at my grandmother's house during my pregnancy. It was one of those quiet days when everyone was out at work, leaving me alone in the house. I remember being in the kitchen, washing dishes, the hum of the faucet the only sound breaking the silence.

As I turned to my left to grab another plate, something caught my eye. Standing right next to me was a boy, maybe 7 or 8 years old. He was dressed in a white gown, and his light skin and brown hair made him look like he had stepped out of a storybook. His brown eyes were wide and full of a kind of innocence and warmth that immediately put me at ease.

There was no sense of fear, no chill running down my spine—just a deep, comforting sense of peace and love. It all happened so quickly, but as I looked at him, a name popped into my mind: Gabriel. It wasn't a sound or a whisper, just a clear impression that this was his name.

I turned to my right, momentarily distracted by something else. When I looked back, he was gone. I didn't know what to make of it, but I felt an overwhelming sense of calm and reassurance.

When my grandmother came home later that day, I eagerly told her about the encounter. My grandma, a devout Christian with a firm belief in the paranormal, listened intently. She told me that what I had experienced was the presence of my guardian angel.

I was curious, though—how could she be so sure? She explained that when you encounter something from the spiritual realm and it fills you with peace rather than fear, it's a sign that the presence is benevolent. If you felt scared or uneasy, that would suggest something darker.

Her words reassured me. The encounter with Gabriel, whoever or whatever he was, left me with a sense of protection and love. It was an experience I would never forget, one that gave me a sense of comfort during a time of change and uncertainty.

Shadow in the Woods

I live in a rural area where farmland once stretched across the landscape, but nature has since reclaimed it. Dense forest now wraps around the old fields, and the undergrowth is thick with thorns, vines, and all sorts of obstacles. There's a trail that I walk frequently; it's the only clear path through the woods. It leads about 150 feet in before ending at a dead end. This trail has been my favorite spot for years. Every morning, I wake up and head straight there, often before I'm even fully awake, just to have a moment of peace.

One day last summer, around 11 a.m., I was on my usual walk. The sun was already high, casting shadows through the trees. Being a typical teenager, I was still groggy and not fully alert. As I approached the end of the trail, I suddenly heard the rustling of the underbrush. The sound was unmistakable—something bipedal moving quickly through the dense foliage. My heart started racing as I turned to locate the source of the sound.

That's when I saw it. About 20 feet past the end of the trail, emerging from the tangled mess of vines and thorns, was a large, black figure. It was so dark it seemed to absorb the surrounding light. It stood at least as tall as me, if not taller. The figure didn't have any distinct features; it was a solid mass of shadow. My instincts kicked in, and I bolted back toward the house, adrenaline fueling my escape.

In the safety of my home, I tried to rationalize what I had seen. Maybe it was just a person who had wandered into the woods where they didn't belong and was startled by my presence. But the speed and the sheer size of the figure made me wonder if it could have been something more—something like Bigfoot, lurking in my own backyard.

Since that day, I've been haunted by the experience. I feel an ever-present sense of paranoia when I walk near the woods. It's as if something—or someone—is always watching me. The woods that used to feel like my own personal retreat now feel alien, as if they belong to something or someone else.

If it was a person, their behavior was unsettling. Why would someone be sneaking through the woods so close to my house, and why would they sprint away when they were caught? The mystery of that encounter has left me with a lingering unease, a feeling that the woods are no longer the safe, familiar place they once were.

Trailer Shadows

I used to live in a four-bedroom, two-bathroom trailer house. It wasn't much, but it was home. For the first six months, it was just me, but then my old roommates moved out, and two new ones moved in. One of them was a woman with whom I eventually started a sexual relationship. She had a peculiar gift —she could see and hear ghosts. As our relationship deepened, I began experiencing things I couldn't explain.

At first, I didn't think much of it. But soon, I started seeing shadowy figures around the house. It was unsettling but intriguing. One afternoon, I was sitting in the corner of the living room while my friend-with-benefits was lounging on the couch, absorbed in a TV show. I was lost in my thoughts when I glanced up and saw a figure standing silently in the doorway, watching her. The figure was indistinct, a dark silhouette against the background, and it gave off an eerie feeling of presence. My heart raced, and I gasped in shock. My friend heard me and turned her head.

"What's wrong?" she asked, her eyes searching mine.

"There's someone standing there, watching you," I managed to say, my voice trembling slightly.

She didn't seem alarmed. "Oh, that's just what happens sometimes," she said calmly. I turned my head back to the spot where the figure had been, but it had already vanished.

The next incident occurred a few weeks later when all of us were gathered in the front room. I was chatting with one of my roommates when I saw a shadow moving out of one of the bedrooms and heading towards us. It was a cat, or at least that's what it looked like—an indistinct shadow with a feline shape. The ghostly cat came within a foot of us before stopping. It seemed to notice that I was watching it, and I could feel its gaze piercing into me.

"What are you looking at?" my roommate asked, noticing my sudden distraction.

I turned to look at her, and then back at the spot where the shadow cat had been. It was gone.

These experiences left me feeling unsettled. They were small moments of strangeness that seemed to shift the normal balance of our lives. I never got used to them, and each encounter left me more curious and anxious than the last. My friend's casual acceptance of the paranormal didn't help to alleviate my growing unease. The shadows in that trailer house became a constant reminder that there were things we could not fully understand, lingering just beyond the edge of our vision.

Midnight Mystery

I'm still trying to piece together what happened that night, and to be honest, I'm not sure if I'll ever understand it fully. Was it a glitch in reality? A bizarre dream? I don't know, but I've never shared this story before, and I'm uncertain if I'm making a mistake by putting it out there now. My name is Diego, and I'm a 29-year-old from Argentina. This incident took place about two years ago, and it remains a mystery I've yet to unravel.

It was early morning, around 2:30 AM, and I was at my computer, just passing the time. Deciding it was time for bed, I took my cell phone and a bag of potato chips to watch an episode of my favorite show. I lay down in bed, opened the streaming app on my phone, found the episode where I left off, and started watching while munching on the chips. I finished both the episode and the bag of chips by around 3:30 AM. Afterward, I closed all the apps on my phone, turned it off, and left the empty bag of chips on my nightstand to throw away the next morning. I got into bed and, after a few minutes, fell asleep.

But then, something strange happened. I woke up to the sound of my phone. When I glanced over, I saw that the episode I had already watched was playing again. The episode was only about 15 minutes into its hour-long runtime. Confused, I checked the time—it was now 4:30 AM. How could this be?

I sat up in bed, bewildered, and noticed something even stranger: the bag of chips, which I had left empty, was now almost full again. It wasn't crumpled or misplaced; it was neatly positioned beside me. My mind raced—had I somehow turned my phone back on while asleep, reopened the streaming app, and resumed watching the episode? How did the bag of chips end up in this state when I remembered clearly eating them all?

The following night, I had a dream unlike any other. I found myself in an unfamiliar place, and a voice spoke to me from above, instructing me not to tell anyone about what had happened the previous night. The dream was unsettling, and the message felt strangely authoritative.

I can't make sense of what happened between 3:30 AM, when I fell asleep, and 4:30 AM, when I woke up. Why did my phone turn on and resume the episode? How did the bag of chips reappear? And what was the significance of the dream urging me to keep quiet?

To this day, two years later, I'm still

searching for answers. It remains one of the strangest and most inexplicable experiences I've ever had, and no matter how much I analyze it, I can't seem to find a rational explanation.

Swinging Hanger

When I was between six and nine years old, my parents had to work long hours, which often left me home alone in our small apartment. It was a cozy place, but when you're a child alone in an empty home, even the smallest sounds can seem amplified.

One day, I was sprawled out on the couch, engrossed in my favorite TV show, the hum of the television filling the room. The sunlight filtered through the small window, casting soft patterns on the floor. I felt safe and content, absorbed in my little world of cartoons and snacks.

Suddenly, my sense of calm was interrupted by a peculiar sight. From my spot on the couch, I noticed a clothes hanger hanging from the hook on the door of the closet in the corner of the room. It was just swaying back and forth. At first, I thought it was a trick of the light or maybe a draft, but I quickly dismissed the idea. It wasn't even summer, so the windows were closed and there was no breeze to speak of.

I sat there, frozen, staring at the hanger as it continued its irregular, swinging motion. The rhythmic movement was completely inexplicable. I tried to rationalize it—perhaps my parents had closed the door too hard before they left, causing it to shift slightly. But that didn't make sense. The door had never been slammed with such force, and even if it had, it would have affected more than just one clothes hanger.

The longer I watched, the more unnerved I became. My tiny heart raced with confusion and fear. I glanced around the room, trying to spot anything else that might explain the phenomenon, but everything else seemed normal. The room was still, and the TV continued to play in its usual monotone drone.

As minutes ticked by, I felt a growing sense of unease. I wanted to call my parents, but I was too young and too scared to think clearly. I finally mustered the courage to approach the closet, determined to stop the hanger from swinging, but as soon as I reached out, it stopped abruptly, as if it had been waiting for me to come closer.

When my parents came home later that day, I hesitated before telling them about the clothes hanger. They brushed it off as a fluke or my imagination. But I remember vividly the eerie calmness of that afternoon and how I felt a shiver run down my spine every time I thought about the swinging hanger.

Years have passed since that day, and the memory has stayed with me. I still wonder what caused that clothes hanger to swing on its own. Was it simply a draft that I missed, or was it something more mysterious? It remains one of those moments in my childhood that I can't quite explain—a fleeting encounter with something inexplicable that left me with more questions than answers.

Unexpected Revelation

Growing up, my family wasn't very religious. My sister and I were taken to church occasionally when we were young, but those visits were brief, and soon we stopped going altogether. For most of my life, I've been an atheist, with moments of agnosticism scattered throughout. I've often found myself dismissing religion, sometimes even making harsh comments about its validity.

Earlier this month, I was at work, my AirPods in, listening to a podcast while I went about my tasks. Music had lost its appeal, and podcasts provided the intellectual stimulation I craved. On this particular day, I was absorbed in an interview with a real-life exorcist. The discussion delved into a world of gods, angels, demons, sin, scripture, and the afterlife. Despite my skepticism, the interview was captivating. It was a world so different from my own, and I found myself oddly engrossed.

During the interview, the conversation touched on a recurring theme: people who, with an open heart, have asked for divine revelation and then experienced something profound. I thought about how many stories like that exist—people who believe that God or some higher power had manifested in their lives in some tangible way.

That same day, I drove home in my father's truck. My own vehicle was out of commission, and I was borrowing his until I could afford to fix mine. Hanging from the rearview mirror was a cross necklace that had belonged to him. It was a simple item, but it held sentimental value for me.

As I drove, lost in thought, the podcast's discussion on divine manifestations still swirling in my mind, something unexpected happened. The cross necklace suddenly came undone and fell from the mirror.

Without even thinking, my hand shot out and snatched the falling cross out of the air. It was a reflexive move, one that felt almost preordained. The necklace had never fallen off before in the time I'd been driving the truck.

In that moment, I was struck by a wave of incredulity. How could it be mere coincidence that on the very day I was contemplating the possibility of divine intervention, the cross fell and I caught it?

As I sat there, holding the cross, my mind raced. Was it a sign? Was it just a fluke?

The moment felt surreal, and I couldn't shake the feeling that there was something more to it. I had always been a skeptic, but this small incident left me questioning if there might be more to the mysteries of the universe than I'd ever allowed myself to believe.

To this day, I'm still not sure what to make of it. But every time I see that cross hanging in the truck, I'm reminded of that strange, inexplicable moment, and it makes me wonder if perhaps, just maybe, there's something out there beyond our understanding.

The Mysterious Disappearance

About a year ago, my mother and I had a strange experience that's left us both puzzled. We were coming off a successful business deal and decided to splurge on some jewelry. My mom prefers to invest in valuable pieces rather than keep money in the bank, so we planned to use cash for the purchase.

We parked in a secure parking lot with surveillance cameras and security personnel. We left a substantial sum of cash in the glove compartment of our car, which we locked securely. We even discussed our usual practice of hiding the money under the glove compartment for extra safety. This wasn't our first time doing this, so we felt confident everything was safe.

After picking out the jewelry, we returned to our car only to discover that the bag of cash was missing. We searched the car thoroughly, checked under every seat, and even went so far as to ask security to review the surveillance footage. They assured us they would investigate, but the whole process took hours. Frustrated and anxious, we ended up filing a police report and went home empty-handed.

When we arrived home, we were astonished to find the missing bag of cash lying on my mom's bed. Everything was intact, just as we had left it. We had no idea how it had gotten there. The last time we saw the bag, it was securely tucked away in the glove compartment of our locked car.

The sight of the cash on my mom's bed

left us both shaken. My immediate reaction was a mix of fear and disbelief. My mom, trying to make sense of the inexplicable, suggested it might be some kind of supernatural occurrence. We were so unnerved by the experience that we decided to donate the money, feeling that perhaps it was a sign or that it was what the spirits wanted.

As time has passed, I've come across theories about glitches in the Matrix or parallel universes. Now, I can't help but wonder if what we experienced was something akin to those theories. Could it be that we witnessed a brief moment of something extraordinary, or was there a logical explanation we missed?

Enigmatic Experiments

In the late 1970s, while I was in kindergarten at Read School in Oshkosh, WI, I experienced something I've never been able to explain. It was an unsettling chapter of my early childhood that has lingered in my memory with an eerie sense of unease.

The school would occasionally take us up to the abandoned third floor, a place that was typically off-limits. The third floor was old and dusty, with turn-of-the-century desks and an old gymnasium that had seen better days. The floor was normally locked due to the presence of bats and an old belltower, but for some reason, we were allowed in on these peculiar occasions.

The visits would begin with us being led to an antiquated classroom. There, we were subjected to a series of strange activities. They would shuffle alphabet cards or a deck of playing cards, lay them face down, and ask us to pick out specific cards. Snacks and juice were provided, and they would play films or scenes on a screen, asking us for our thoughts. We wore headphones and participated in various tests, though I could never recall the specifics of these activities.

One particular day, my mother was informed by a supposed teacher—someone who wasn't a regular staff member—that I had picked out all the alphabet cards in order, something that was deemed impossible. My mother was shocked, especially since I had been taken out of my regular kindergarten class and didn't seem to remember anything about the visit. After the juice and snacks, I would often feel disoriented and off-kilter upon returning to class.

As the years passed, I've always felt an instinctive discomfort about those experiences. My mother mentioned that the individuals running these sessions were associated with the nearby University of Wisconsin-Oshkosh, though their exact role or purpose was never clear. The secrecy of it all, combined with the disorienting effects I felt afterward, has led me to suspect that something was amiss. The idea that I might have been drugged or subjected to some sort of experiment feels like the most plausible explanation, especially since several other children were involved in these mysterious sessions.

Now, over 45 years later, the memory still unsettles me. There was something profoundly wrong about the secrecy and the strange activities we were subjected to. It feels as though something significant was hidden from us, and I can't shake the feeling

that there was more to those sessions than I—
or anyone else—ever knew.

Phantom Encounter

Eighteen years ago, I was with three friends on our way to a party. It was around 11 or 12 at night, and we hadn't been drinking or using any substances. We were driving through a quiet stretch of road when we pulled up to a stop sign. The driver, unsure of which direction to take, was consulting with one of the friends in the front seat, trying to figure out our route.

As we sat there, waiting, I glanced to the

right and saw something strange on the road. About 15 yards away—close enough to make out a shape but too far to see details clearly— was what looked like a dog on all fours. My attention was briefly caught, but I shifted my focus back to the front seat as my friends debated our next move.

Out of the corner of my eye, I noticed the creature suddenly stand up. It was then that I fully focused on it, and a chill ran down my spine. I couldn't keep silent. I screamed, "What the hell is that?!" My friends turned to look, their faces going pale as they took in the sight.

The creature was about three and a half feet tall, its knees bent inward in an unnatural way. As it started walking toward us, it moved under a streetlight, but its features were disturbing—there were no eyes, no mouth, nothing but a solid black silhouette. It was an opaque, formless entity.

Panic set in, and we sped away from the stop sign, glancing back as we fled. The creature appeared to follow us, but its deformed legs seemed to hinder its movement, making its chase awkward and ineffective.

This encounter has haunted me for years, and we didn't discuss it much afterward. We all eventually lost touch, but a few years ago, I reached out to the friend who had been driving. I messaged him, saying, "Hey, remember that night when we were lost looking for that party?" His immediate response was, "And we saw that thing in the road that tried to chase us?"

I've often wondered what we saw that night. The inward-bent knees of the creature are what unsettled me the most. If anyone else has encountered something similar or can shed light on what this could have been, I'd appreciate your insight. For reference, I live in East Tennessee, USA.

Strange Experience in North Carolina

I've never been a strong believer in the paranormal—more of a skeptic, really. But a recent vacation with my girlfriend turned out to be unsettling enough to make me reconsider. We had planned a week-long stay in North Carolina, followed by a trip to Florida to visit some old friends of mine. However, two days into our North Carolina stay, we decided to cut our trip short and return to Europe because of a series of strange, unexplainable events.

To keep things brief, we had rented a large cabin on a farm/ranch in North Carolina. The first night was uneventful until my girlfriend suddenly woke me up. She was panicked, hitting me and accusing me of tampering with her underwear while she slept. I was confused and insisted that I was sound asleep and had no idea what she was talking about. I didn't believe her at the time, which I regret deeply and have apologized for many times since.

The following night, after a full day of ziplining and physical exhaustion, we went to bed early around 10:30 PM. Normally, I don't dream or remember my dreams, but in the middle of a deep sleep, I was jolted awake by what felt like my father's voice shouting my name. My father had passed away two years prior, so hearing his voice was particularly unsettling. The room was silent, and the weather outside was calm.

Still shaken, I turned to check on my girlfriend. To my shock, I found her underwear had been pulled loose, though still covering her, and there were scratches on the inside of both of her legs—scratches that hadn't been there earlier. I tried to convince her that I had nothing to do with it, but she initially thought I was responsible and was understandably distressed. She decided to take a shower to calm down, and it was around 3 AM by then.

Confused and worried, I called my mom to explain what had happened. Her theory was that my father's voice might have been a warning because he sensed something malevolent around us. Although I'm skeptical of such explanations, my girlfriend is now convinced that we need to seek help from a priest or a medium.

Since that night, nothing else unusual has occurred, but my girlfriend hasn't slept well. She doesn't blame me for the incident, but the experience has left us both unsettled.

Toilet Teleportation

I have to share this strange experience my husband had recently; it's truly baffling. We were at an outlet mall, and I decided to pop into Starbucks to charge my phone for a bit. I settled into a chair right next to the restrooms, a spot where I had a clear view of the entrance. There was no way anyone could slip past me without being seen—they would have to walk directly in front of me, and I'd have a clear sightline to the rest of the area the moment they came out.

My husband went to use the restroom, and I watched him walk towards it. From where I sat, I had a full view of the Starbucks, including the counter, the main seating area, and a large table with about five people working on their laptops. I was absorbed in my phone when something astonishing happened.

Out of the corner of my eye, I noticed my husband seemingly appear out of nowhere and land on the floor near the large table. At first, it looked like he had fallen, but it was impossible for him to have gotten there without passing in front of me. I leaped up, rushing to him, my heart racing. He looked incredibly shaken and immediately said, "That was crazy. Let's go."

It took him several minutes to calm down and gather his thoughts. When he finally spoke, his voice was shaky as he recounted what had happened. According to him, he went into the restroom, used the facilities, and washed his hands. Then, while he was leaning against the wall, the next thing he knew, he was on the floor in the main seating area of Starbucks, where I had seen him fall.

He couldn't explain how he got there, nor could he remember walking out or moving at all. It was as if he had vanished from the restroom and reappeared in the dining area without any sense of transition. We left the mall immediately, and though we tried to make sense of it, the experience has left us both bewildered. It felt like something out of a sci-fi movie, and we're still trying to figure out how such a bizarre thing could happen.

Unsettling Visitor

I'm currently on vacation with my dad, trying to relax and enjoy the break, but an unsettling experience has cast a shadow over my trip. It all started with a text from my mom early one morning, around 6 a.m. She was just checking in, but the message she sent was anything but ordinary.

The night before, my stepdad had ventured downstairs in the middle of the night for a drink or a snack. He was groggy but distinctly remembered seeing someone standing in the dark kitchen. The figure looked just like me, though I was supposed to be on vacation. He assumed I had come home earlier than planned. The figure merely glanced at him, smiled, shrugged, and walked away into the darkness. To him, it was nothing more than a weird coincidence—he didn't think much of it, chalking it up to a late-night mix-up.

It wasn't until the next morning that he realized something was amiss. I had left my door open, but I wasn't in my room. Alarmed, he asked my mom if I had left with friends or perhaps returned earlier. She looked puzzled and told him that I had been away the entire time and had never come home. My stepdad insisted that he had seen someone who looked exactly like me, and his insistence only heightened my mom's worry.

The situation took a creepier turn when my mom mentioned that we have cameras installed around the house, but ironically, they were undergoing updates that night. No footage from the night in question was available.

My mom was understandably concerned and, given the circumstances, texted me right away to make sure I was okay. She feared the figure my stepdad saw might have been something supernatural—my ghost, perhaps—and wanted to ensure I was safe.

Now, as I'm still away, I can't shake off the feeling of dread about returning home. I have no idea what to expect or how to interpret what happened. Is there a symbolic meaning behind this unsettling occurrence? Should I be worried about something more sinister? This is the first time anything like this has happened, and I'm left with a gnawing uncertainty about what awaits me when I get home.

The Unsettling Apartment

I used to live in an old apartment building that had been erected sometime in the 1970s or '80s. From the moment we moved in, the place seemed to have an air of unease about it, and over the years, I experienced a series of unsettling occurrences that I've never been able to fully explain.

The first incident happened when I was around seven years old. At that age, I was deeply afraid of the dark, so I'd often end up sleeping in my mom's room for comfort. One night, I woke up abruptly without any discernible reason. I began scanning the room with my wide, curious eyes, and that's when I saw her.

Above my mom's dresser was a large, circular mirror. Reflected in its surface was the figure of a woman draped in a veil. Her attire resembled a Victorian mourning dress, with dark, flowing fabrics that seemed almost antique. I stared at her for what felt like an eternity, my young mind trying to grasp the reality of what I was seeing. Despite my fear, I eventually fell back asleep, unable to comprehend the vision before me. To this day, I have no logical explanation for the apparition. It couldn't have been a shadow because nothing in the room had shifted, and there was no way someone could have been outside the window since we lived on the second floor.

A few months later, I encountered more strange presences in my mom's room. The first was an old man who appeared to be a relic from another era. He wore a white coat and carried a cane, but his face was horrifyingly disfigured, as if it had been melted or scarred beyond recognition. The second entity was a teenage girl with blonde hair. She wore blue jeans, a red sweater, and white sneakers. Her face was always hidden, and she was often seen crying inconsolably. Despite my attempts to approach her and offer comfort, she would vanish whenever I tried to look at her face or reach out to touch her.

The most unsettling experience occurred when I was about thirteen. I was lying in bed, struggling to fall asleep when I suddenly felt a weight settle on my leg. I assumed it was my mom coming to check on me, but when I looked, the bed was empty. I lay there frozen, hiding beneath my blankets until the weight lifted, leaving me both frightened and confused.

Another strange incident involved the building's intercom system. This system was fairly rudimentary—there was no microphone, just a way to buzz specific apartments. When someone buzzed an apartment, the person inside would press their own button to grant access.

One day, after school, I came home and realized I had forgotten my key. I buzzed our apartment, and the door was unlocked when I arrived. I thought my mom had let me in, so I went inside looking for her. However, she wasn't there. I called her phone, only to find out she was still at work—she had never left. She rushed home in a panic, but the apartment was empty. No one had been inside except me, and I still have no idea who had let me in or unlocked the door.

Each of these incidents has left me with more questions than answers, and despite trying to rationalize them, I can't help but feel that something inexplicable was at play in that old apartment.

Whispers in the Shadows

My family and I once lived in an old brick bungalow in Saudi Arabia, nestled amidst the harsh desert landscape. My father was an architectural engineer working for Raytheon, designing and constructing facilities for foreign employees and testing compounds. His work brought us into close contact with the powerful elite of the region —wealthy Emirs swimming in oil and luxury, who were, in essence, the real rulers of the land. These men, dressed in their immaculate white thobes, would visit our home to discuss business with my father. They were always polite and would bring gifts for me and my siblings, though I was too young to grasp the full gravity of their true nature. My father later revealed that these seemingly benevolent men were ruthless powerbrokers, surrounded by spies and enforcers, involved in toppling governments and manipulating conflicts across the Middle East and Africa.

When I was about six years old, we moved to Canada, leaving behind the arid expanses of the desert for a more temperate climate. We settled into a spacious bungalow with a sandy yard in a quiet neighborhood. The area was sparsely populated with other homes, most of which were occupied by individuals associated with the Saudi Royal Family. The few empty houses nearby became my playgrounds—places I explored when I sought to escape the confines of our home.

My mother, deeply rooted in Middle Eastern traditions, frequently warned us about the Djinn. She described them as shape-shifting entities capable of appearing in various forms: shadows, monstrous beings with hooved feet, or even as ordinary humans capable of mimicking voices. Her tales were meant to instill caution, especially about abandoned houses, which she believed were likely inhabited by these trickster spirits. According to her, unexplained noises, misplaced objects, and eerie occurrences were the work of the Djinn.

One night, when I was three, my mother had a chilling experience. Driven by an unsettling feeling, she entered my room to check on me. There, in the corner near my bed, she saw a dark shadow—a shape that seemed almost alive. The moment she flipped on the light, the shadow vanished. Terrified for my safety, she spent several nights in my room and eventually had a holy man cleanse the space. After that, the shadows ceased to appear, and she seemed reassured.

As I grew older and we settled into our new life in British Columbia, I thought the supernatural tales were behind me. However, when I was seventeen, I had an experience that shook me to my core. One night, I awoke in my bed, paralyzed and unable to move. To my horror, a shadowy figure with glowing red eyes sat in a chair beside me. The figure seemed to radiate malevolence. Though it had no visible mouth, I could sense a sinister grin. The figure's presence filled me with sheer terror as I struggled against my paralysis, making only muted, anguished noises.

The shadow man seemed to revel in my fear. He sat there, red eyes locked onto me, until he suddenly stood up with a chilling, guttural laugh. He swiftly moved towards my brother's room down the hall, leaving behind streaks of red light. As soon as he was gone, my paralysis lifted. Shaken, I went to the kitchen for water, trying to convince myself it had been a vivid dream.

But as I drank, I heard the same muffled screams I had made earlier. They were coming from my brother's room. I rushed over and found him in the same state of paralysis I had experienced. Over him was a dark, ominous cloud, and he too was moaning in silent terror. When he woke, he described the shadow man with red eyes—exactly as I had seen him.

Stunned by the coincidence, we shared our experiences and could only wonder how this malevolent entity had managed to torment both of us in such a synchronized manner. My brother, who had never taken my mother's warnings seriously, was now faced with an unsettling reality that he couldn't ignore. The experience left us both shaken, and even though my brother had never shown interest in the paranormal, he was deeply affected by the encounter.

The next day, we told our mother about the incident. She was immediately reminded of her own terrifying encounter in Saudi Arabia and took it as a sign of Djinn presence. Determined to protect us, she performed rituals and prayers to cleanse our home of any lingering malevolent forces. While this seemed to bring some peace, the shadowy figures never completely disappeared from my life.

In the years that followed, I continued to experience occasional sightings of shadow figures, though never with the same intensity or malevolence as that first encounter. I would catch glimpses of them darting in my peripheral vision or appearing briefly in darkened rooms. Over time, I came to accept these encounters as part of my reality, attributing them to the Djinn or similar entities that live on the fringes of our world.

Through my research, I discovered that Djinn, like us, live complex lives and can be both benign and malevolent. They have their own beliefs, duties, and forms of existence, often manifesting as shadows because it's a form our minds can comprehend. While my experiences with them have faded, the memory of that night with the shadow man remains a stark reminder of the thin veil between our world and theirs.

Phantom on Creek Road

I'm twenty-four now, but I still remember the eerie events of that night when I was about fifteen, in the tenth grade. My friends and I had been invited to a party hosted by one of our classmates. The party was held in a neighborhood known for its rough edges—rural, low-income, and unfortunately, a hotbed for local drug activity. This detail would prove to be crucial as the night unfolded into something out of the ordinary.

The neighborhood had a reputation, and as soon as we pulled into the area, a collective shiver ran down our spines. There was something off about it—something that made our skin crawl. It wasn't necessarily dangerous, just unsettling and dark. We tried to brush off our unease, attributing it to the dimly lit streets and the foreboding ambiance of the surroundings.

The party itself was uneventful, but as the night wore on, the strange feeling persisted. We were all a little tipsy from drinking, but no one was drunk. After a while, we decided it was time to head home. We packed ourselves into my friend's car, eager to leave the unsettling neighborhood behind.

As we drove through the winding streets, the sense of dread grew stronger. The darkness seemed to swallow the houses, and the shadows seemed to move of their own accord. We were spooked, but we kept rationalizing it as nerves from the dark and unfamiliar area.

We came to a stop at an intersection, waiting for the light to change. It was around 2 a.m., and the street was eerily quiet. Out of nowhere, a woman appeared on the sidewalk to our right. She was walking her dog, or at least that's what it looked like at first glance. The neighborhood was deserted, and her sudden appearance felt jarring.

She was dressed in an old-fashioned coat, and her face was unnervingly blank—no emotion, no expression. What was most unsettling was her mannerisms. As she walked along the sidewalk, she seemed almost detached from reality. She lifted her right foot high in the air as if preparing to take a step off the curb and towards the street. Her mouth opened wide in a grotesque, unnatural way, as if her jaw was unhinging to an impossible degree.

My friends and I stared in horrified silence, our eyes glued to the strange figure. Before we could process what was happening, my friend, who was driving, slammed his foot on the gas pedal. We sped away from the stop sign, not daring to look back to see if she had followed us. The car was filled with nervous chatter as we drove in silence, each of us trying to make sense of the encounter.

When we finally arrived at my friend's house, we were all visibly shaken. The fear had united us, and we decided to spend the rest of the night on the basement couch, huddled together. None of us slept well, haunted by the image of the woman with the unearthly gaze and the disturbing, unhinged jaw.

The next day, we discussed the night's events, trying to rationalize what we had seen. Some suggested that the woman might have been on drugs, explaining her strange behavior and appearance. Others, including me, wondered if we had witnessed something supernatural—an encounter with a spirit or an apparition.

To this day, I'm not sure what we saw that night. The memory of the woman on

Creek Road, with her hollow gaze and unsettling mannerisms, remains vivid. It's a reminder that sometimes the most unsettling experiences are those that defy explanation, leaving us with more questions than answers.

Phantom on the Ceiling

My daughter, who's only two years old, has a curious habit that's begun to unsettle me. She has this endearing quirk where she points at any man she sees—on TV, in pictures, or in person—and calls him "Dada." It doesn't matter if the man looks nothing like her father; to her, all men are "Dada."

Lately, this peculiar habit has taken on a new twist. She often points up at the ceiling above my bed, exclaiming "Dada!" with the same enthusiasm she reserves for her father. This has happened at all times of the day— mornings, afternoons, and nights. Whether the room is bathed in daylight or shrouded in darkness, she seems to see something on that ceiling that eludes me.

I've tried to investigate what she might be pointing at. I've scrutinized the ceiling for any shapes or shadows that could resemble a man, but there's nothing discernible. The ceiling is just a plain, white expanse with no discernible patterns or anomalies. Yet, every time she points up there and says "Dada," there's a certain conviction in her tiny voice that makes me wonder if she's seeing something I can't.

There's another aspect to her behavior that adds to the unease. When she senses tension or sadness in the room, she has this habit of fake laughing. It's almost as if she's trying to lighten the mood by forcing herself to laugh, hoping that her laughter will spread to those around her. It's a sweet gesture, though it sometimes feels a bit misplaced.

Recently, she's directed this behavior towards the ceiling. On a couple of occasions, when she's pointed up and said "Dada," she's accompanied it with her signature forced laughter. It's both endearing and unsettling. It's as if she's trying to coax a response or cheer up an unseen presence.

Despite the oddity of the situation, I'm not particularly frightened. I don't believe anything harmful is happening, but the whole experience is undeniably strange. It's as though there's an invisible presence that only my daughter can perceive, and it's become a topic of intrigue and mild concern for me.

As I watch her gaze up at the ceiling and call out "Dada," I can't help but feel a mixture of curiosity and wariness. The idea that something might be lingering in the shadows above us is both fascinating and unsettling. I've shared this story because it's a bizarre situation that's left me pondering the nature of what my daughter might be seeing.

Whether it's a figment of her

imagination, a playful spirit, or something else entirely, I find myself hoping for an explanation. Until then, the phantom on the ceiling remains a mysterious presence in our home, observed only by my little girl and her innocent, unwavering gaze.

A Mysterious Vision

For as long as I can remember, I've had a peculiar experience where vivid images appear in my mind without any conscious effort on my part. These are not dreams, but rather, day-dreams or visualizations that seem to come from nowhere. This phenomenon intensified a few years ago, and I've often wondered if these images are somehow connected to my unconscious mind.

One incident stands out as particularly

strange, and the more I think about it, the weirder it becomes. A few years ago, while visiting a large city, I was resting in bed, not quite asleep but not fully awake either. As I lay there, a startlingly vivid image materialized in my mind. It was a woman's face, staring directly at me. She had blondish hair, a pale complexion, and appeared to be in her twenties. What was truly unsettling was a specific physical feature she possessed—one that I couldn't recall ever seeing in anyone else. The feature was so unique that it gave me an eerie feeling, making her look like something straight out of a horror movie.

Despite the unsettling nature of the image, I felt a pang of sympathy for her and wondered if there was a way I could help, though the fear lingered. The next day, while riding the train, I turned around and was confronted by a startling sight. There, standing in front of me, was the exact same woman from my visualization. She had the same blondish hair, the same pale complexion, and, most disturbingly, the same unique feature that had so unnerved me.

Instinctively, I moved away from her, trying to escape the discomfort of being observed by someone who had just haunted my mind the previous night. My gut feeling was one of unease, and I couldn't shake the sense of foreboding.

At the time, the coincidence felt somewhat strange but not entirely out of the ordinary. I brushed it off as an odd but isolated incident. However, upon reflection, it seems far more bizarre and difficult to rationalize.

One scientific explanation that comes to mind is that I might have seen this woman in the city earlier without consciously noticing her. My brain could have registered her presence, and then the image surfaced during my rest. But this would have required an entirely subconscious observation, as I am certain I had never seen her before that moment.

Alternatively, it could be that the image was purely random, and the sighting of this exact person was a coincidence. Yet, given the strikingly unique feature and the fact that the visualization was the only one I had that night, the coincidence seems implausible. Why would my mind conjure such a specific image of a person I had never met, only for that exact person to appear the very next day?

The encounter remains one of the most inexplicable and eerie experiences I've had, leaving me with more questions than answers. The coincidence, if it can be called that, has haunted my thoughts, adding a layer of mystery to an otherwise ordinary day.

The Enigmatic Hill

This story has lingered in my mind for years, and despite the length and possible errors in my account—English isn't my first language—I feel compelled to share it. Back in my childhood, around 2011-2014, when I was about 7 or 8 years old, I experienced something that nearly drove me to the edge of sanity. It affected my ability to sleep, focus, and even led to academic failure. I lost friends who thought I was losing my grip on reality. I'm now reaching out to understand what might have happened, or if anyone else has experienced something similar.

Growing up, I had a close-knit group of friends: Mark, Leo, and Sam. We were inseparable, despite Mark being somewhat of a troublemaker. We lived in a small city with a predominantly rural feel, and one day, after school, we decided to explore. It was around 5 or 6 PM when we set out.

Our first stop was an old playground. After a while, we decided to head to a newer playground. For reasons I can't quite recall, possibly Mark's suggestion, we ended up trespassing onto someone's yard. I'll refer to it as the "red gate" due to its proximity to a red gate.

We pushed through dense bushes, crossed a small river, and eventually came upon train tracks—something I was unaware existed in our city. These tracks were out of service and not commonly known, so their presence was baffling.

After what felt like 20 minutes, we emerged from the foliage into a scene straight out of a fairy tale. To our left was a small pond, and the grass was a vivid green, contrasting sharply with the previously brownish landscape.

My memory gets fuzzy from here, but I recall we climbed a large hill from which we could see our city from above. The view was astonishing and disconcerting. Our city, which should have been modern, appeared old-fashioned with brick and wood buildings. The landscape lacked any cars or contemporary elements. There was a large church with an unusual symbol on its roof instead of the standard cross. It resembled either a crescent moon, a star, or a logo I found online.

Sam, who had strict parents, checked his watch and panicked, realizing we were late. He insisted we needed to leave or face severe consequences.

Here's where things become even more

strange. I have no recollection of how we got home or what happened next. I remember nothing from that day to when I was around 11 or 13 years old. It's as though my memory of that period is entirely blank, except for fragmented memories like the name of a teacher.

Years later, I asked my friends about that day when I was 11. Leo and Mark recalled it, though their memories were vague. Sam, however, said he didn't remember much beyond a fuzzy recollection of being on a hill.

When I turned 15, I asked them again if they remembered the incident. They looked pale and insisted they didn't know what I was talking about. They seemed worried and thought I was losing my grip on reality. Sam, although he believed me, advised me not to revisit the area, suggesting that if what we experienced was real, it might be better left unexplored.

Eventually, we lost touch. When I reached out to them two years ago to discuss the experience again, they denied ever talking about it and suggested I might have dreamed it. I rarely remember dreams, and this memory feels far too vivid and unusual to be a mere dream.

I've since distanced myself from those friends, fearing they would think I'm mentally unstable. My new friends either believe me or pretend to. I'm considering returning to the location with my new group to seek answers.

Key Points to Consider:

1. I didn't know about the train tracks beforehand, ruling out the possibility of it being a dream.

2. My friends initially remembered the event, though their recollections grew hazy over time.

3. Mark was always a troublemaker.

4. I've had similar eerie experiences in this town, possibly of a paranormal nature.

5. I'm mentally sound, with no family history of schizophrenia or other mental illnesses.

If anyone has experienced something like this or has any insight into what might have happened, I would greatly appreciate your thoughts.

A Devil in Florence

My encounter with something unspeakable happened in Florence, and though the tale might seem mundane at first glance, the raw, primal fear I experienced is forever etched in my memory. I was there on vacation with my family—my parents, my sister, and I. It was evening, and the soft, yellow glow of the streetlights cast long shadows beside a high, ancient wall as we strolled along the sidewalk.

We were enjoying ourselves, sharing lighthearted jokes, when we noticed a figure approaching us from the opposite direction. He was a young man, clad in a gray hoodie with the zipper pulled up and the hood obscuring his face. His hands were buried deep in his pockets, and he walked with a quick, purposeful stride, his head lowered and eyes fixed on the ground.

As he drew closer, I stole a glance beneath the shadow of his hood. I glimpsed his face for no more than a couple of seconds, yet that fleeting moment was enough to sear an image into my mind that has haunted me for nearly a decade. The terror I felt in that instant was unlike anything I had ever experienced—primordial, almost instinctual, as if my very being recognized him as a primal threat. It was as though he had existed since time began as a predator lurking in the dark corners of human consciousness.

The man's appearance defied any rational explanation. His skin was covered in tawny, glossy fur reminiscent of a beaver's pelt, and his face was grotesquely elongated into a downward-bent snout, devoid of whiskers. His eyes, tiny and jet-black like marbles, were unnervingly vacant. Even now, as I recount this, I shiver at the memory, and the sensation of cold dread creeps up my spine.

I tried to catch my breath as he passed by, my heart pounding. I turned to look at him again, my mouth agape, feeling the cold sweat on my back and the hair standing up on my arms. I told my family what I had seen, my voice trembling and my words stumbling over themselves. My description fell short of capturing the true horror I had felt, and I had no proof to offer skeptics beyond the palpable fear that still grips me whenever I think of that night.

There was no conventional explanation for what I saw—no photograph, no visual evidence, nothing online that matched the creature I encountered. The terror that man carried with him was more than fear; it was an overwhelming, pervasive dread that has left a permanent mark on my psyche.

Enigmatic Light on the Arizona Road

In the spring of 1996, my grandfather handed me a well-worn map, tracing a route from Seattle to Sedona. The purpose of the journey was straightforward: I was heading to the spring training for the Mariners. The dawn had yet to break as I began my drive through the flat, sprawling landscape of Arizona. The road stretched out endlessly before me, a perfect canvas for introspection and daydreaming.

As I cruised along, lost in thought, an

unexpected phenomenon interrupted the serene solitude. A light appeared on the horizon, so intense and brilliant it seemed to defy the laws of nature. It pierced through the darkness with an almost supernatural quality. The light was so blinding that it felt as though it was not merely illuminating the road but searing through me, leaving an indelible mark on my senses. The brightness was so vivid that even in my peripheral vision, it appeared to burn through the darkness, leaving a surreal imprint in my memory.

The next clear moment I recall, I was standing outside the ticket booth at the baseball stadium in Sedona. Despite the routine nature of spring training, tickets still had to be purchased. As I stood there, disoriented and confused, it was as if a significant chunk of time had vanished without explanation. I found myself in a daze, trying to piece together what had happened.

Suddenly, my reverie was interrupted by the sound of my name being called urgently from across the fence. "KARYL! KARYL!"

The voices, familiar yet distant, jolted me out of my trance. I looked up to see a group of friends on the other side of the fence. Their presence brought a rush of clarity. They asked if I had a ticket, to which I replied, "No, I was just trying to figure out..."

Before I could finish my sentence, one of them said, "I have an extra ticket for you."

The game was set to start at 2 PM, and I had left home at 5 AM. The hours that had passed between my departure and my arrival were a blur. I had no recollection of where I had parked my car or how I had managed to cover the distance so quickly. My friends had to assist me in locating it, their puzzled expressions mirroring my own bewilderment.

The entire experience left me with a lingering sense of disorientation and a profound sense of lost time. The memory of that blinding light remained vivid, casting a shadow over the rest of my journey. It was as if I had briefly stepped out of reality, only to return with no clear explanation for the gap in my perception.

Green-Eyed Woman

Since 2014, I have been haunted by a recurring figure in my dreams—a woman with piercing green eyes who appears in various guises and roles. Her presence has spanned several years, surfacing again in 2017 and 2018, each time as a different person but always retaining those unsettling, emerald eyes. These dreams are unlike any ordinary fantasy; they feel more like echoes of past lives, where I find myself inhabiting the bodies of different people, spanning across various historical eras.

In the initial encounter, the green-eyed woman appeared in a dream as a distant figure. When I asked her name, she simply told me it wasn't time yet. As the years progressed, she seemed to draw closer, evolving from an enigmatic acquaintance into a friend or even a caregiver, like a hospice nurse. Despite her shifting roles, those piercing green eyes remained a constant, unsettling presence.

Then, in 2017, reality seemed to blur with my dreams. I met a woman in real life who had the same striking green eyes. She quickly became my best friend, a connection I initially cherished. Despite my reservations due to past betrayals, I invested deeply in this friendship, eager to overcome my fears. However, as time passed, I found myself growing increasingly uncomfortable. Her mannerisms, subtle yet disconcerting, made me uneasy, casting a shadow over our bond.

By mid-2019, her life took a drastic turn. She found herself trapped in an abusive relationship and a hostile environment, or at least she became more open about her struggles. I tried to support her through these turbulent times, even though I was grappling with my own difficulties. Yet, our friendship seemed to evolve into a one-sided affair. She began using me as her emotional outlet, neglecting my own needs and boundaries. I felt as though I was being emotionally manipulated and abandoned, a painful echo of previous experiences.

What made things even worse was the restriction she imposed on our conversations. She forbade me from discussing anything related to my past, current political issues, or global news. Our topics of discussion were limited to subjects she enjoyed, such as "Lord of the Rings" and various anime, interests I had little affinity for. Despite my attempts to accommodate her preferences, the narrowing of our conversation topics further strained our relationship.

In retrospect, I can't help but think that these recurring dreams featuring the green-eyed woman were more than mere coincidences. They might have been warnings or omens about the nature of this friendship. Perhaps there is a karmic connection at play, suggesting that our past lives were intertwined in ways that have resurfaced in this lifetime.

Ultimately, I believe the green-eyed woman in my dreams was a harbinger, forewarning me of the challenges and troubles that this friendship would bring. Her presence, consistent yet shifting through my dreams and reality, may have been an attempt to prepare me for the emotional turbulence that lay ahead. What do you think? Could this enigmatic figure be a signal of unresolved past connections or a premonition of the difficulties I would face?

Revelation in the Twilight

The afternoon sun cast long shadows across our living room as my father, once a robust and formidable figure, now appeared frail and diminished. His health had been deteriorating for months, and seeing him shrink into a shell of his former self was a painful reality to confront. I could barely watch as he lost weight, his once strong frame now withered and weak. It was as if I was witnessing the slow extinguishing of a flame that had once burned so brightly.

It was during one of those dreary days that he sat down in his favorite armchair—a place he used to occupy with a commanding presence. His face was a mask of confusion and fear, and he told us he thought he might be having a stroke. As he spoke, his voice trembled, and he kept muttering to himself about death. It was as if he was locked in a battle with the specter of mortality, challenging it with every ounce of his remaining strength.

"You don't scare me, you son of a bitch," he shouted at the empty air, his words echoing through the room, leaving us bewildered and anxious. None of us knew how to respond or even what was happening. My mother stood silent, her face ashen and her eyes wide with a mix of terror and disbelief. My brother and I exchanged uneasy glances, unsure of how to handle this sudden and frightening turn of events.

Then, in a moment that took us all by surprise, my father began talking about feeling euphoric. He described experiencing altered states of consciousness, recalling how, in his days as a doctor, he would sometimes enter these states while working. It was as if he was trying to communicate something profound, something beyond the grasp of everyday understanding.

When my father turned to my mother, trying to share his thoughts, she was rendered speechless, her fear rendering her mute. It was clear she couldn't comprehend what he was experiencing, and her silence was almost as loud as his outbursts. I was right there beside him, and when he asked my brother about his intellectual interests, my brother mentioned his passion for video games. My father's response was a curse muttered under his breath, a clear sign of his disappointment.

My mother, desperate for some form of communication, urged my father to speak with me. He rarely paid much attention to me, and our conversations were almost non-existent. But on this day, he turned to me with a mixture of hope and desperation in his eyes. I told him I understood what he was going through, and as I spoke, I saw a wave of relief wash over him. It was as if he had been waiting for someone to truly understand him, and in that moment, he finally found it in me.

We began discussing complex topics—individuation, Jung versus Freud, quantum physics, and the divide between the physical and spiritual realms. It felt like an awakening for both of us. For the first time, I felt truly heard, and I could sense that my father was experiencing a moment of clarity. It was a rare connection, bridging the gap that had long existed between us.

Our political and religious differences had often led to heated arguments. He was a Southern conservative, deeply entrenched in his Catholic faith, and his dedication to both often led to contentious debates with my mother. His past alcoholism had cast a long shadow over my childhood, leaving me with deep scars and fears. The memory of his volatile temper and the threat of violence was never far from my mind. His admission of having once hired someone to harm his ex-girlfriend, though it never came to fruition, only added to the trauma.

For years, it felt like we were living in separate worlds, our interactions limited to mere coexistence. Conversations were rare, and our interactions were often marked by silence or tension. The barrier between us seemed insurmountable, each of us trapped in our own isolated universe.

But that day marked a turning point. Seeing my father calm down from his earlier delirium and relax as he ate ice cream was both comforting and unsettling. He revealed something that shook me to my core: he believed this experience ran in the family. He recounted how his grandmother had spoken of seeing heaven, a revelation that struck a chord with me. Just a week earlier, I had experienced something similar—an encounter with what I believed to be the afterlife, a vision that was both beautiful and terrifying.

I had cried bitterly upon waking, overwhelmed by the profound sense of love and truth I had encountered. It was a revelation that left me feeling both elated and despondent, knowing that such profound love was beyond the reach of our earthly existence. It was a bittersweet realization that we could not fully experience the love we were capable of on this plane.

This shared experience of mystical visions and altered states made me reconsider my entire perception of my family and myself. I had always felt like an outsider, convinced that my unique experiences and feelings set me apart from my family. To discover that my father had similar experiences was both comforting and disconcerting. It was as if a door had been opened, revealing a connection that had been there all along, hidden beneath layers of misunderstanding and fear.

My mother, still in shock, asked me if my father was crazy. Her dismissal of his experience as schizophrenia hurt deeply. I knew that if he was crazy, then I was too, for I understood and felt the reality of these experiences. I tried to explain, but the sense of dread and anxiety lingered.

As I lay awake the following morning, I felt a deep, gnawing anxiety, a sense of foreboding that I couldn't shake. Witnessing my father's struggles and his apparent surrender to death made me reflect on my own fears and vulnerabilities. I saw in him a reflection of my own anxieties—hidden, repressed, and slowly consuming us both.

The realization that we were both hiding our true selves and our gifts was a painful one. It made me confront the possibility that I too might be living a life of self-denial, hiding my own light and potential. I couldn't bear the thought of following the same path, of succumbing to the slow poison of self-repression.

I retreated to the bathroom, tears streaming down my face, grappling with the weight of this revelation. No one knew about my anguish, and I was left alone with my thoughts. I still don't know how to navigate this new understanding or what to do with these insights. But the story of my father and the glimpse into our shared struggles is a bittersweet one, a reminder of the unspoken connections that bind us.

I hope that one day, I can honor this newfound understanding and make us proud, finding a way to embrace and share the gifts we both have kept hidden.

Haunting of the Old Lobby

In the bustling suburbs of Shanghai, where the skyline tells tales of relentless development, I found myself in one of the city's oldest, most forgotten corners. This area, once a hub of crumbling hovels, had transformed over the past forty years into a landscape of sleek luxury apartments. Located near the old airport, it was among the first places redeveloped when China began its sweeping modernization in the late 20th century. Amidst the new, some buildings from the early 1990s still stood, their faded facades a whisper of the past.

One rainy evening, as the downpour intensified, I decided to take shelter in an empty building lobby that had always intrigued me. The structure, circular in design, hinted at its former life as a bustling restaurant. Now, it stood as a forgotten relic, shrouded in darkness and dust.

I ventured into the lobby, its once bright interiors now dim and forlorn. The circular shape of the space seemed to draw me toward a well-lit hallway that spiraled into a dark stairwell. The dimness of the stairwell contrasted sharply with the faint glow of the hallway, and there was an eerie 'dead' area beneath the first flight of stairs that caught my attention. Curiosity nudged me to explore further.

As I entered the stairwell, an oppressive sense of dread washed over me. The sensation was so intense that it felt as though an invisible force was screaming in my mind, urging me to leave. The darkness around me seemed to pulsate with malevolent energy, and I could see nothing but shadows.

Suddenly, a vision burst into my mind—a girl, covered in blood, crouched on the floor, her sobs echoing through my thoughts. The sheer terror of the image made my heart race, and I instinctively backed away from the stairwell. My eyes darted around, trying to make sense of the overwhelming fear, but the vision persisted, vivid and disturbing.

I stumbled out of the stairwell and hurried down the curving hallway, glancing back to see if anything followed me. The hallway remained empty, but the feeling of being pursued lingered. I sensed the girl's presence trailing behind me, an invisible weight that seemed to halt at the door as I rushed outside.

My escape was frantic, driven by an irrational but overpowering fear. As I walked away from the building, my mind was still reeling from the vivid images and the deep-seated dread I had felt. I had never considered myself particularly sensitive to supernatural occurrences, but the fear and the vision of the bloodied girl had felt alarmingly real.

The experience left me shaken, and I couldn't shake the feeling that something unsettling was trapped within the walls of that old lobby. Whether it was the echoes of a tragic past or a lingering presence, I couldn't say. All I knew was that I had encountered something in that building that night—a haunting that defied explanation and left me with a chilling sense of unease.

Mysterious Cat and the Girl from Romania

For nearly two decades, I've wrestled with the inexplicable memory of an event that unfolded during my fifth grade, an enigma that has lingered in my mind despite my best efforts to rationalize it. The story begins with a girl named Bai, who I met during my early years in a bustling apartment complex in Shanghai.

Bai was a few grades younger than me,

having moved to Shanghai from Romania not long before we met. She had a striking feature: her eyes were a mix of brown and blue, a condition called heterochromia, with half of one iris shimmering a vivid blue. This detail would later become crucial to understanding the bizarre series of events that transpired.

Bai's family was unlike any I had encountered. Her apartment was filled with unsettling decor: candles, strange altars, and an assortment of taxidermy. Her mother was particularly secretive and distressed whenever Bai's friends visited, so we usually had to sneak in and out when her mom was away shopping. My own mother, pregnant and often unwell, had never met Bai or been inside her apartment.

Despite the odd atmosphere surrounding Bai's home, I found her to be a kindred spirit. Many kids avoided her, feeling uneasy for reasons they couldn't articulate. Perhaps it was the strange aura of her family or the enigmatic beliefs they followed. Bai shared that her family practiced a belief system similar to paganism but not quite like any of the more common spiritual practices I had heard of. Her claims of possessing special powers intrigued and skeptical me, so I challenged her to prove it.

To my astonishment, Bai agreed to demonstrate her abilities. She told me she would transform into a cat and visit me that very night. I dismissed it as an idle boast, not giving it much thought. My family lived on the third floor of our apartment building, with no fire escapes or balconies—just narrow window ledges that barely accommodated a plant pot.

That night, I wore a pair of Care Bear pajamas, a gift from my mother, and went to bed as usual. Around 3 a.m., I was jolted awake by a persistent scratching sound at my window. Groggily, I got out of bed and peered outside, my heart racing. There, on the impossibly thin window ledge, sat a black cat. The cat's eyes were eerily familiar—it had one eye that was half blue, just like Bai's.

The cat raised its paw in a peculiar gesture, almost as if it were waving at me. Terrified, I convinced myself it was just a dream and went back to sleep.

The next morning, as my mom cooked breakfast, she brought up something unusual. "I heard scratching at the window last night. When I checked, there was a black cat on the ledge, trying to get inside. I was worried it might fall, so I brought it in and then let it out downstairs. It had one eye that was half blue —I've never seen a cat like that before."

A chill ran down my spine. I could hardly speak, my breakfast sitting untouched on my plate. I didn't know how to respond, especially when my mom's description matched exactly with what I had seen.

Later that day, Bai approached me, addressing me with the nickname "Gloomy Bear." "Hey, why didn't you let me in last night?" she asked casually.

I was stunned into silence.

"I could have died! At least your mom was kind enough to help me out," Bai added, her tone eerily nonchalant.

Our friendship didn't last much longer after that. A few weeks later, a fire broke out in our building, forcing us to move to a different town. Bai and I lost touch, and I never saw her again.

To this day, my mom occasionally reminisces about the strange cat with the half-blue eye, still baffled by how it could have perched on our narrow window ledge. For twenty years, I've grappled with the memory, searching for a logical explanation, but nothing fits. The incident remains one of the strangest, most inexplicable experiences of my life, a haunting reminder of the night when reality and the supernatural seemed to blur beyond recognition.

The Day I Saw a UFO

I understand if you're skeptical, but I need to share this because it's impossible to talk about with my friends or family. I'm not into spreading tall tales online; I just want to recount what happened to me without facing ridicule. Online trolls don't bother me, but the thought of my loved ones thinking I've lost my mind does.

Here's my story:

It was a beautiful afternoon, the kind where everything seems perfect. The sky was a flawless blue, and the temperature was just right at about 75 degrees. I was out for a jog, enjoying the weather, when suddenly, a blinding red flash erupted in the sky. It was so intense that it made me squint and flinch. When I looked up, I saw something that defied all my expectations of what a UFO should look like.

For about 15 to 20 seconds, my brain struggled to process what my eyes were seeing. Above the trees just ahead of me was a massive, beige-colored triangular aircraft. It was enormous—easily as long as two or three passenger jets—and it hovered silently. The aircraft was flanked by three brilliant balls of light: two behind it and one in front, all arranged in a triangular pattern. The light from these orbs was so intense that it was impossible to make out any details; it was like staring directly at the sun.

The underside of the triangular craft had three enormous lights: two red and one white.

These lights rotated in a synchronized sequence—first one red light would flare up, then dim, followed by the second red light, and then the white one. This sequence continued throughout the encounter. The lights were not coming from traditional bulbs; they seemed to be emanating from voids or open spaces in the craft, like starlight streaming out from a darkened sky.

What struck me as odd was that, as I watched, all sounds abruptly ceased. I could no longer hear the traffic or the usual ambient noise. The colors around me— the green of the grass and the blue of the sky—appeared more vivid, almost unnaturally so. It felt like I was standing on a raised platform, even though I knew I was on solid ground. The sensation was akin to standing on a pitcher's mound, with everything else appearing distant and detached.

As I stood there, trying to make sense of it all, I noticed a man on a bicycle approaching the craft from behind me. I tried to shout at him, but he seemed to be moving in slow motion. Although he was only about 30 to 50 yards away, it felt like it took minutes for him to cover that distance. He never acknowledged me or appeared to notice the UFOs.

Then, to my left and higher up in the sky, another beige triangle suddenly materialized out of nowhere. It blinked its lights simultaneously, then vanished and reappeared, repeating the light sequence as it did. It didn't fly in or out; it just appeared and disappeared. The experience felt like an acknowledgment of each other's presence, though I'm aware how odd that sounds.

After that strange moment, normalcy returned. The sound came back, the colors reverted to their usual shades, and I felt firmly back on the ground. The triangular craft began to ascend slowly, taking about 5 to 7 minutes to disappear completely from view. I could still see its rotating lights high in the sky as it moved away. The whole encounter lasted around 12 minutes.

When I turned around, I noticed two police vehicles about 200 yards away. Their windows were heavily tinted, and they definitely weren't there when I first arrived. I hurried away, and they didn't follow or get out of their vehicles.

You can believe whatever you want, but I know what I saw. It felt like a deeper, more profound experience than just an extraterrestrial visit. Thanks for letting me share this anonymously.

A Night to Remember: The Bicester UFO Incident

Twelve years ago, in Bicester, UK, I had an experience that has stuck with me ever since. At the time, I was just 14 years old, and UFOs or aliens were far from my mind. I had never given them a second thought, but out of nowhere, I found myself inexplicably drawn to the idea of spotting UFOs. It was a sudden fascination that I couldn't shake.

The next evening, I convinced some of

my family members to join me in the garden. It was a clear night, perfect for stargazing. We settled in and chatted for about ten minutes when I noticed something odd. A dim white light, resembling a spotlight but dull in color, appeared in the sky. It looked as if it were attached to something, shaped like an oval, which was how I could tell it was connected to an object.

The light drifted silently over the houses to our left and came to a halt right in front of us, about 100 feet in the air and 200 feet away. That's when things got really strange.

I felt a sudden, intense sensation in my chest, like a surge of adrenaline, but without the usual physical symptoms. It was as if time and space had warped around me. I was fixated on the light, yet it felt like my consciousness was detached from my body, unable to fully grasp the situation.

In an instant, the light brightened, and what happened next defied explanation. It accelerated at an unbelievable speed, reaching what I can only describe as 20,000 mph. There was no sound, just an astonishingly swift movement.

I lost sight of the light momentarily but then looked up and saw it high above, now tiny and distant like a star. It shot off into space, leaving a faint trail of light behind it, reminiscent of a comet.

My family remained silent throughout the entire event. Once it was over, we exchanged glances, unable to articulate what we had just witnessed. The fear and disbelief were palpable; none of us could fathom the reality of what we had seen.

The Black Cube Encounter: A Haunting Experience

In 2011, I had an encounter that has forever changed my life. I was working in networking at the time, and my hours often stretched late into the night. I'd usually get off work around 2 a.m., and after a few hours of winding down, I'd head to bed.

One particularly rainy evening, I had just finished my shift and made my way home through a torrential downpour. By the time I arrived, the rain had let up, so I decided to step outside for a quick smoke. I was talking on the phone with a friend about work while I stood in the damp, cool air.

It was still drizzling lightly, and low-lying clouds covered the sky. The orange street lights in Allen cast an eerie glow, reflecting off the bottom of the clouds and creating an almost artificial illumination. A strong breeze whipped around, but the rain had stopped.

As I faced west, something caught my eye. To my right, moving from the north and heading south at about 60 to 80 mph, was a massive black cube. It was traveling with one corner pointed forward. The sheer size of it was astonishing—it looked to be 80 to 100 feet tall.

The cube had a rough, stone-like surface and appeared to be entirely black. On one of its sides, there was a border surrounding what looked like a circular maze. The sight was both mesmerizing and disturbing. As it moved, it disturbed the air around it, leaving a spinning vaporous trail that quickly dissipated.

What struck me most was the utter silence. Despite its size and speed, there was no sound—none at all. It moved steadily in the direction of southbound 75 Central Expressway towards downtown Dallas.

In disbelief, I tried to describe what I had seen to my friend who lived a few miles south. I was so flustered that I could barely find the words. I urged him to go outside and see if he could spot it. He ventured out into his street, scanning the sky in the direction of my sighting. After about five minutes, the rain returned, and he stood outside for another 15 minutes but saw nothing.

People have ridiculed me and questioned my sanity since that night, but I know what I saw. The cube appeared to be carved from a single piece of stone, with a distinct circular pattern on its surface—like looking at a maze from above. There were no lights on the craft, which was surprising; I had expected some sort of light show but was nonetheless amazed by what I witnessed.

I've been searching for information on "black cube UFOs" ever since, every single day. The experience has haunted me, and I can't shake the desire to see it again. It's a relief to finally share this and get it off my chest.

February 2020: A Mysterious Encounter in Central Arkansas

In February 2020, I was out with a friend on his grandparents' farmland, located about 15-20 minutes outside our town in Central Arkansas. We often spent weekends there, building fires and enjoying the outdoors with a few friends. This particular weekend, it was just the two of us.

It was dark by the time we arrived. We

set up a fire on the dirt path that ran from the house, through the field, and towards the woods. We built the fire in the center of the field and settled in with some music and beers.

After a short while, my friend noticed something unusual in the sky behind me (my back was to the woods). He turned off the music and pointed it out. There was a bright light above the treeline. While it was unusual to see a star so bright, neither of us was too concerned initially. I pulled out a stargazing app on my phone, thinking it might be a planet. But before I could get a good look, the light began to move.

We both froze. The light glided smoothly to the right, moving quickly and silently. It became clear that it was not a star but some kind of flying vehicle. The craft was much closer than we initially thought—probably 300 to 400 feet away, flying just above the treetops. Despite its speed, it moved silently, which seemed strange.

The bright light emanating from the side of the craft obscured our view, but we could tell it was dark and difficult to identify. It flew parallel to the treeline and seemed to notice we were watching it. It continued in a straight line, quickly disappearing from sight within seconds.

We exchanged incredulous glances, trying to process what we had just seen. About twenty minutes later, the peaceful night was interrupted by the sound of two loud planes flying side by side, heading in the same direction the light had gone. We speculated that the object we saw might have been a military drone.

After that, the night was quiet. We didn't see or hear anything else. The encounter left us puzzled and curious, but the sight of the planes gave us a possible explanation, even if we were left with more questions than answers.

My Encounter with the Men in Black: A Story from 2004

A Prelude to the Unusual

In 2004, my life took a turn that I could never have predicted. The incident that set everything into motion happened during a camping trip to Joshua Tree National Park with a few friends. On our last night there, we gathered around the campfire, gazing up at the clear night sky, captivated by the vast expanse of stars.

As we were staring at the heavens, two glowing blue objects suddenly appeared. They zipped across the sky at incredible speeds, maneuvering in ways no aircraft should be able to. My friends and I were left speechless, utterly amazed and mystified. I tried to capture the moment with my flip phone, but the objects moved too fast to get a clear image. Despite our excitement, we had no evidence to show for it.

On the drive back home, we couldn't stop talking about what we had seen. The excitement was palpable, but it was quickly overshadowed by an unsettling realization: a black car was following us. I switched lanes multiple times, trying to shake it off, but the car stayed with us, maintaining a constant distance. Then, as suddenly as it appeared, the car vanished without a trace. The eerie incident left us all on edge.

The Encounter

The next day, after running a few errands, I drove home and saw a black Cadillac parked in my driveway. My stomach churned with unease. Could it be the same car that followed us yesterday? I tried to convince myself otherwise, but my instincts told me I was right.

As I stepped out of my car, two men approached me. They wore identical black suits, light gray dress shirts, black ties, and black fedoras. Their appearance was unsettling—almost plastic and expressionless, with pale olive skin tones. Their eyes were cold and intense, and they spoke in raspy, monotone voices, their speech unnervingly precise and synthetic.

"We'd like to ask you a few questions about what you witnessed last night," one of them said.

"Who are you?" I asked, trying to steady my voice. "Can I see some credentials?"

"We work for a division of the US Air Force," the other replied, showing me a badge that looked official enough but didn't quite quell my doubts.

Their questions were direct and probing:

- "Can you describe what you saw that night?"

- "What do you think you saw?"

- "Did you take any photos of what you witnessed?"

- "Were there others who might have had recording devices or cameras?"

- "Do you know if anyone recorded the incident?"

- "Have you spoken about this incident

with anyone else who wasn't present with you that night?"

- "Did you find any unusual debris at the location you were that night?"

- "Would you be withholding any important information from us?"

I answered as evasively as I could, withholding many details about what I saw and who I was with. I didn't trust these men, and their presence felt ominous.

The interrogation concluded with a chilling warning: "We strongly advise you to refrain from talking about what you witnessed with anyone and to forget the incident ever happened. We'll be keeping an eye on you in case you decide to ignore our advice."

The Aftermath

For weeks, I felt a constant sense of unease, always looking over my shoulder, expecting to see the black Cadillac again. The encounter with those men haunted me, and I became hesitant and careful about sharing my experience.

In the years that followed, I had a few more UFO sightings, but they were fleeting and less dramatic. Thankfully, I haven't had any more visits from men in black suits—at least, not yet.

Sharing this story now, I hope to shed light on what I experienced and perhaps connect with others who might have gone through similar encounters. Whether these men were truly part of some secret government agency or something else entirely, I'll never forget the fear and confusion they instilled in me. My experience with the Men in Black remains one of the most surreal and disturbing events of my life.

A Nightly UFO Encounter: An Unforgettable Experience

My mother and I have always been fascinated by aliens and UFOs. Her interest stemmed from a wild firsthand experience she had when she was younger, but that's a story for another time. The first time we saw mysterious lights in the sky, it was still an insane experience to witness firsthand. Now, seeing these lights has become a nightly occurrence. There have only been a handful of times when we haven't seen anything.

Let me get into it, because I'd love to know if anyone else has had similar sightings!

When we first noticed these distant, bright moving lights, I said, "It's probably a satellite." But that explanation quickly fell apart when they started performing maneuvers. We were shocked at how fast they moved, often slowing down only to zip forward or backward, sometimes in a zigzag pattern across the sky. These movements were often small but exaggerated, occasionally involving very wide movements up and down. On one occasion, we saw two light sources almost chasing one another, speeding up and performing complex maneuvers, darting across the sky, disappearing, and then reappearing.

I would have continued to shrug these off as satellites if it weren't for their speed, movements, and patterns.

One night, I spotted one that seemed to have multiple light sources. It's hard to explain, but it was almost as if it had lights all around it that would turn on and off in different spots. These lights were still far enough away that they could be dismissed as stars, but the movement of the lights around it was noticeable, even without my glasses on!

While this may not be the most wildly out-there story, I'd love to hear if anyone else has had similar experiences. For us, these nightly sightings have become a captivating mystery that continues to fuel our fascination with the unknown.

The Hat Man: A Haunting Warning

I only have one experience with the Hat Man, but it's something I'll never forget. I was 14 years old, and it happened one night after I had just put my phone down and laid in bed. My room was in the basement, and I was staring into the darkness. There were no lights on whatsoever, yet he was even darker —darker than the darkness itself.

Suddenly, I saw the Hat Man. He was

wearing a wide-brimmed hat and a long trench coat. He was void of all features, a shadowy figure moving past my bed and into the other room in the basement. Terrified, I slammed my eyes shut and eventually fell asleep.

The next morning, I was talking to my younger brother, who was only a few months younger than me. He told me that the night before—the same night I saw the Hat Man— he saw a dark man, darker than the shadows in his room, just standing there.

I have a theory that the Hat Man is associated with mirrors. Not long before my brother and I both saw the Hat Man, we had experienced something strange in the bathroom. While we were in the showers, we both received writing on the mirror. I'm not quite sure what his said, but mine said, "Get out" or "Get out of this house," or something very close to that. I always showered with the door shut and took very hot showers, so I would have noticed if someone walked in because the cold air would have flooded in.

Another theory is that the Hat Man might be a warning. At the time, I was living with both of my moms and four of my siblings. Three of my siblings were Mom A's, and one of them, along with me, was Mom B's. A few months after I saw the Hat Man, Mom B, my sibling, and I moved out. Mom A's boyfriend moved in with her and the other three siblings. Maybe a year later, Mom A's boyfriend got drunk and killed her, one of my sisters, and my brother who also saw the Hat Man. He shot the other sister, but she survived. Tragically, the others, including Mom A's boyfriend who shot himself, did not survive.

I believe the Hat Man could possibly be a reaper, but most importantly, a warning. A warning that something very bad is going to happen. Indeed, something very bad did happen.

The Stalker

When I was around 19, I had a chilling encounter I've never forgotten. I'm 33 now, and it's still my only experience with him.

Back then, I lived in an apartment with my ex, Andrew. He worked night shifts at a gas station, so he wasn't home from 10 pm to 6 am. I always slept with a night light because ever since I was a kid, I'd get nightmares or my mind would play tricks on me, making me paranoid about seeing things in the dark, I often felt like I was being watched. When I shared a bed with someone, I never had this problem, but alone, I always needed a light on.

One night, I was lying on my back in our bedroom. I remember this vividly. I opened my eyes and looked up at the ceiling, seeing our bedroom exactly as it was. To this day, I don't know if I was awake or dreaming. I hadn't had dreams that realistic before in my own room. It might have been my first experience with sleep paralysis because I've had it frequently since.

As I lay there, I heard the creaking sound of the cheap linoleum floor in the apartment. It was the same sound it made when someone stepped on it, especially near the dishwasher. I felt like someone was in the kitchen, walking towards the room, and the air seemed to shift. I thought to myself, "Oh, Andrew is home." But then, near my left shoulder, I heard a deep voice say, "No, it's me."

In my peripheral vision, I saw a man in a black bowler hat with pale white skin and a black collared trench coat that covered half his face. He didn't look shadowy, but he did seem dark except for his pale skin. I must have woken up then because Andrew wasn't there. He was still at work when I texted him about the nightmare. I couldn't sleep; I was too terrified because the dream felt so real.

When Andrew came home, I told him what happened. He said, "Oh, so you saw the hat man, too." I've read a lot of stories about top hats and fedoras, but this man definitely wore a bowler hat. It's been 13 years, and I can still remember every detail of that encounter.

Share Your Supernatural Story with Bald and Bonkers Network LLC!

Have you experienced something that defies explanation? Do you have a story that's been burning inside, waiting to be told? Bald and Bonkers Network LLC invites you to be part of our groundbreaking video and anthology series, **"Why We Are Supernatural."**

We're calling on all truth-seekers, paranormal enthusiasts, and anyone who's ever had a brush with the unknown to share your true stories with us. Your experiences could be featured in our upcoming anthology book or even spotlighted in our documentary series!

How to Submit:

Email: Send your story to **bbwhywearesupernatural@gmail.com**

What We're Looking For:

True stories about encounters with the

supernatural—whether it's ghosts, unexplained phenomena, or anything that's left you questioning the boundaries of reality.

Why Share? By sharing your story, you're not only contributing to a community of like-minded individuals but also helping others find the answers they're searching for. Together, we can shed light on the mysteries that unite us all.

Don't miss this chance to have your voice heard and your story immortalized. Whether it's an eerie encounter or a life-changing event, we want to hear from you!

Join Us in Exploring the Unknown— Submit Your Story Today!

For more details, visit Bald and Bonkers Network LLC.